SPEED THE PLOUGH

CW01497523

Bird College
dance, music and theatre performance

7 Station Road, Sidcup, Kent DA15 7EB
Tel: 020 8300 6004
Fax: 020 8308 1370
Email: performance@birdcollege.co.uk
Website: www.birdcollege.co.uk

SPEED THE PLOUGH

Thomas Morton

www.General-Books.net

Publication Data:

Title: Speed the Plough
Author: Morton, Thomas, 1764-1838
Reprinted: 2010, General Books, Memphis, Tennessee, USA

How We Made This Book for You
We made this book exclusively for you using patented Print on Demand technology.
First we scanned the original rare book using a robot which automatically flipped and photographed each page.
We automated the typing, proof reading and design of this book using Optical Character Recognition (OCR) software on the scanned copy. That let us keep your cost as low as possible.
If a book is very old, worn and the type is faded, this can result in numerous typos or missing text. This is also why our books don't have illustrations; the OCR software can't distinguish between an illustration and a smudge.
We understand how annoying typos, missing text or illustrations, foot notes in the text or an index that doesn't work, can be. That's why we provide a free digital copy of most books exactly as they were originally published. You can also use this PDF edition to read the book on the go. Simply go to our website (www.general-books.net) to check availability. And we provide a free trial membership in our book club so you can get free copies of other editions or related books.
OCR is not a perfect solution but we feel it's more important to make books available for a low price than not at all. So we warn readers on our website and in the descriptions we provide to book sellers that our books don't have illustrations and may have numerous typos or missing text. We also provide excerpts from books to book sellers and on our website so you can preview the quality of the book before buying it.
If you would prefer that we manually type, proof read and design your book so that it's perfect, simply contact us for the cost. Since many of our books only sell one or two copies a year, unlike mass market books we have to split the production costs between those one or two buyers.

SPEED THE PLOUGH

SPEED THE PLOUGH;
A COMEDY,
IN FIVE ACTS;
AS PERFORMED AT THE
THEATRE ROYAL, COVENT GARDEN.
By
THOMAS MORTON, Esq
.

PRINTED UNDER THE AUTHORITY OF THE MANAGERS FROM THE PROMPT BOOK.
   WITH REMARKS
   BY MRS. INCHBALD.
LONDON:
PRINTED FOR LONGMAN, HURST, REES, AND ORME,
PATERNOSTER ROW.
   SAVAGE AND EASINGWOOD,
PRINTERS, LONDON.

REMARKS.

This comedy excites that sensation, which is the best security for the success of a drama–curiosity. After the two first acts are over, and pleasantly over, with the excellent drawn characters of Ashfield and his wife, and the very just satire which arises from Sir Abel's propensity to modern improvements–the acts that follow excite deep interest and ardent expectation; both of which are so highly gratified at the conclusion of the play, that, from the first night of its performance, it has ranked among the best of the author's productions, and in the first class of modern comedies.

The various characters of this play are admirably designed, but not so happily finished as the author meant them to be–witness, Bob Handy, who begins a self-conceited coxcomb, and ends a tragedy confidant.

But the good intentions of an author are acceptable: execution will not always follow conception; and the last may often give as much instruction, though not equal delight with the former: as an instance, who does not see the folly of attempting to *do every thing* in Handy, though he is more the shadow, than the substance of a character.

Notwithstanding there are some parts, not so good as others, in this comedy, there is no one character superior to the rest, nor any one in particular, which makes a forcible impression on the memory:–this proves, (in consequence of the acknowledged merit of the play) the fable to be a good one, and that a pleasing combination has been studied and effected by the author, with infinite skill, however incompetent to his own brilliant imagination.

The plot, and serious characters of this comedy, are said to be taken from a play of Kotzebue's, called, "The Duke of Burgundy,"–if they are, Mr. Morton's ingenuity of adapting them to our stage has been equal to the merit he would have had in conceiving them; for that very play called, "The Duke of Burgundy," by some verbal translator,–was condemned or withdrawn at Covent Garden Theatre, not very long before "Speed the Plough" was received with the highest marks of admiration.

The characters of Sir Philip Blandford, his brother, and his nephew, may have been imported from Germany, but surely, all the other personages of the drama are of pure English growth.

The reception of this play, when first performed, and the high station it still holds in the public opinion, should make criticism cautious of attack–but as works of genuine art alone are held worthy of investigation, and as all examinations tend to produce a degree of censure, as well as of praise, "Speed the Plough" is not exempt from the general lot of every favourite production.

An auditor will be much better pleased with this play, than a reader; for though it is well written, and interspersed with many poetical passages, an attentive peruser will find inconsistencies in the arrangement of the plot and incidents, which an audience, absorbed in expectation of final events, and hurried away by the charm of scenic interest, cannot easily detect.

The most prominent of these blemishes are:–Miss Blandford falls in love with a plough-boy at first-sight, which she certainly would not have done, but that some preternatural agent whispered to her, he was a young man of birth. But whether this magical information came from the palpitation of her heart, or the quickness of her eye, she has not said.–A reader will, however, gladly impute the cause of her sudden passion to magic, rather than to the want of female refinement.

The daughter has not less decorum in love, than the father in murder.–That a character, grave and stern, as Sir Philip Blandford is described, should entrust any man, especially such a man as Bob Handy, with a secret, on which, not only his reputation, but his life depended, can upon no principle of reason be accounted for; unless the author took into consideration, what has sometimes been observed,–that a murderer, in contrivance to conceal his guilt, foolishly fixes on the very means, which bring him to conviction.

PERSONS REPRESENTED.

Sir Philip Blandford
Mr. Pope.
Morrington
Mr. Murray.
Sir Abel Handy
Mr. Munden.
Bob Handy
Mr. Fawcett.
Henry
Mr. H. Johnston.
Farmer Ashfield
Mr. Knight.
Evergreen
Mr. Davenport.
Gerald
Mr. Waddy.
Postillion
Mr. Abbot.
Young Handy's Servant
Mr. Klanert.
Peter
Mr. Atkins.

Miss Blandford
Mrs. H. Johnston.
Lady Handy
Mrs. Dibdin.
Susan Ashfield
Miss Murray.
Dame Ashfield
Mrs. Davenport.

SPEED THE PLOUGH.
ACT THE FIRST.
SCENE I.

In the fore ground a Farm House.–A view of a Castle at a distance.

Farmer Ashfield
discovered at a table, with his jug and pipe.
   Enter Dame Ashfield
, in a riding dress, and a basket under her arm.

Ash. Well, Dame, welcome whoam. What news does thee bring vrom market?

Dame. What news, husband? What I always told you; that Farmer Grundy's wheat brought five shillings a quarter more than ours did.

Ash. All the better vor he.

Dame. Ah! the sun seems to shine on purpose for him.

Ash. Come, come, missus, as thee hast not the grace to thank God for prosperous times, dan't thee grumble when they be unkindly a bit.

Dame. And I assure you, Dame Grundy's butter was quite the crack of the market.

Ash. Be quiet, woolye? always ding, dinging Dame Grundy into my ears–what will Mrs. Grundy zay? What will Mrs. Grundy think–Canst thee be quiet, let ur alone, and behave thyzel pratty?

Dame.–Certainly I can–I'll tell thee, Tummas, what she said at church last Sunday.

Ash. Canst thee tell what parson zaid? Noa–Then I'll tell thee–A' zaid that envy were as foul a weed as grows, and cankers all wholesome plants that be near it–that's what a' zaid.

Dame. And do you think I envy Mrs. Grundy indeed?

Ash. Why dant thee letten her aloane then–I do verily think when thee goest to t'other world, the vurst question thee ax 'il be, if Mrs. Grundy's there–Zoa be quiet, and behave pratty, do'ye–Has thee brought whoam the Salisbury news?

Dame. No, Tummas: but I have brought a rare wadget of news with me. First and foremost I saw such a mort of coaches, servants, and waggons, all belonging to Sir Abel Handy, and all coming to the castle–and a handsome young man, dressed all in lace, pulled off his hat to me, and said–"Mrs. Ashfield, do me the honour of presenting that letter to your husband."–So there he stood without his hat–Oh, Tummas, had you seen how Mrs. Grundy looked!

Ash. Dom Mrs. Grundy–be quiet, and let I read, woolye? [*Reads.*] "My dear farmer" [*Taking off his hat.*] Thankye zur–zame to you, wi' all my heart and soul–"My dear farmer"–

Dame. Farmer–Why, you are blind, Tummas, it is–"My dear father"–Tis from our own dear Susan.

Ash. Odds dickens and daizeys! zoo it be, zure enow!–"My dear feyther, you will be surprized"–Zoo I be, he, he! What pretty writing, bean't it? all as straight as thof it were ploughed–"Surprized to hear, that in a few hours I shall embrace you–Nelly, who was formerly our servant, has fortunately married Sir Abel Handy Bart."–

Dame. Handy Bart.–Pugh! Bart. stands for Baronight, mun.

Ash. Likely, likely,–Drabbit it, only to think of the zwaps and changes of this world!

Dame. Our Nelly married to a great Baronet! I wonder, Tummas, what Mrs. Grundy will say?

Ash. Now, woolye be quiet, and let I read–"And she has proposed bringing me to see you; an offer, I hope, as acceptable to my dear feyther"–

Dame. "And mother"–

Ash. Bless her, how prettily she do write feyther, dan't she?

Dame. And mother.

Ash. Ees, but feyther first, though––-"As acceptable to my dear feyther and mother, as to their affectionate daughter–Susan Ashfield."–Now bean't that a pratty letter?

Dame. And, Tummas, is not she a pretty girl?

Ash. Ees; and as good as she be pratty–Drabbit it, I do feel zoo happy, and zoo warm,–for all the world like the zun in harvest.

Dame. Oh, Tummas, I shall be so pleased to see her, I shan't know whether I stand on my head or my heels.

Ash. Stand on thy head! vor sheame o' thyzel–behave pratty, do.

Dame. Nay, I meant no harm–Eh, here comes friend Evergreen the gardener, from the castle. Bless me, what a hurry the old man is in.

Enter Evergreen

Everg. Good day, honest Thomas.

Ash. Zame to you, measter Evergreen.

Everg. Have you heard the news?

Dame. Any thing about Mrs. Grundy?

Ash. Dame, be quiet, woolye now?

Everg. No, no–The news is, that my master, Sir Philip Blandford, after having been abroad for twenty years, returns this day to the castle; and that the reason of his coming is, to marry his only daughter to the son of Sir Abel Handy, I think they call him.

Dame. As sure as two-pence, that is Nelly's husband.

Everg. Indeed!–Well, Sir Abel and his son will be here immediately; and, Farmer, you must attend them.

Ash. Likely, likely.

Everg. And, mistress, come and lend us a hand at the castle, will you?–Ah, it is twenty long years since I have seen Sir Philip–Poor gentleman! bad, bad health–worn almost to the grave, I am told.—What a lad do I remember him–till that dreadful– [*Checking himself.*] But where is Henry? I must see him–must caution him–[*A gun is discharged at a distance.*] That's his gun, I suppose–he is not far then–Poor Henry!

Dame. Poor Henry! I like that indeed! What though he be nobody knows who, there is not a girl in the parish that is not ready to pull caps for him–The Miss Grundys, genteel as they think themselves, would be glad to snap at him–If he were our own, we could not love him better.

Everg. And he deserves to be loved–Why, he's as handsome as a peach tree in blossom; and his mind is as free from weeds as my favourite carnation bed. But, Thomas, run to the castle, and receive Sir Abel and his son.

Ash. I wool, I wool–Zo, good day. [*Bowing.*] Let every man make his bow, and behave pratty–that's what I say.–Missus, do'ye show un Sue's letter, woolye? Do ye letten see how pratty she do write feyther.

[*Exit.*

Dame. Now Tummas is gone, I'll tell you such a story about Mrs. Grundy–But come, step in, you must needs be weary; and I am sure a mug of harvest beer, sweetened with a hearty welcome, will refresh you.

[*Exeunt into the house.*

SCENE II.

Outside and gate of the Castle–Servants cross the stage, laden with different packages.

Enter Ashfield

.

Ash. Drabbit it, the wold castle 'ul be hardly big enow to hold all thic lumber.

Sir Abel Handy. [*Without.*] Gently there! mind how you go, Robin.

[*A crash.*

Ash. Who do come here? A do zeem a comical zoart ov a man–Oh, Abel Handy, I suppoze.

Enter Sir Abel Handy

.–Servant

following.

Sir Abel. Zounds and fury! you have killed the whole county, you dog! for you have broke the patent medicine chest, that was to keep them all alive!–Richard, gently!–take care of the grand Archimedian corkscrews!–Bless my soul! so much to think of! Such wonderful inventions in conception, in concoction, and in completion!

Enter Peter

.

Well, Peter, is the carriage much broke?

Peter. Smashed all to pieces. I thought as how, sir, that your infallible axletree would give way.

Sir Abel. Confound it, it has compelled me to walk so far in the wet, that I declare my water-proof shoes are completely soaked through. [*Exit* Peter

.] Now to take a view with my new invented glass!

[*Pulls out his glass.*

Ash. [*Loud and bluntly.*] Zarvent, zur! Zarvent!

Sir Abel. [*Starting.*] What's that? Oh, good day.–Devil take the fellow?

[*Aside.*

Ash. Thankye, zur; zame to you with all my heart and zoul.

Sir Abel. Pray, friend, could you contrive *gently* to inform me, where I can find one Farmer Ashfield.

Ash. Ha, ha, ha! [*Laughing loudly.*] Excuse my tittering a bit–but your axing mysel vor I be so domm'd zilly [*Bowing and laughing.*]–Ah! you stare at I beceas I be bashful and daunted.

Sir Abel. You are very bashful, to be sure. I declare I'm quite weary.

Ash. If you'll walk into the castle, you may zit down, I dare zay.

Sir Abel. May I indeed? you are a fellow of extraordinary civility.

Ash. There's no denying it, zur.

Sir Abel. No, I'll sit here.

Ash. What! on the ground! Why you'll wring your ould withers–

Sir Abel. On the ground–no, I always carry my seat with me [*Spreads a small camp chair.*]–Here I'll sit and examine the surveyor's account of the castle.

Ash. Dickens and daizeys! what a gentleman you wou'd be to shew at a vair!

Sir Abel. Silence fellow, and attend–"An account of the castle and domain of Sir Philip Blandford, intended to be settled as a marriage portion on his daughter, and the son of Sir Abel Handy,–by Frank Flourish, surveyor.–Imprimis–The premises command an exquisite view of the Isle of Wight."–Charming! delightful! I don't see it though [*Rising.*]–I'll try with my new glass–my own invention–[*He looks through the glass.*] Yes, there I caught it–Ah! now I see it plainly–Eh! no–I don't see it, do you?

Ash. Noa, zur, I doant–but little zweepy do tell I he can zee a bit out from the top of the chimbley–zoa, an you've a mind to crawl up you may zee un too, he, he!

Sir Abel. Thank you–but damn your titter. [*Reads.*]–"Fish ponds well stocked"–That's a good thing, Farmer.

Ash. Likely, likely–but I doant think the vishes do thrive much in theas ponds.

Sir Abel. No! why?

Ash. Why, the ponds be always dry i'the zummer; and I be tould that bean't wholesome vor the little vishes.

Sir Abel. Not very, I believe–Well said surveyor! "A cool summer house."

Ash. Ees, zur, quite cool–by reason the roof be tumbled in.

Sir Abel. Better and better–"the whole capable of the greatest improvement."–Come, that seems true however–I shall have plenty to do, that's one comfort–I have such contrivances! I'll have a canal run through my kitchen.–I must give this rustic some idea of my consequence. [*Aside.*] You must know, Farmer, you have the honour of conversing with a man, who has obtained patents for tweezers, tooth-picks, and tinder boxes–to a philosopher, who has been consulted on the Wapping docks and the Gravesend tunnel; and who has now in hand two inventions which will render him immortal–the one is, converting saw dust into deal boards, and the other is, a plan of cleaning rooms by a steam engine–and, Farmer, I mean to give prizes for industry–I'll have a ploughing match.

Ash. Will you, zur?

Sir Abel. Yes; for I consider a healthy young man, between the handles of a plough, as one of the noblest illustrations of the prosperity of Britain.

Ash. Faith and troth! there be some tightish hands in theas parts, I promize ye.

Sir Abel. And, Farmer, it shall precede the hymeneal festivities–

Ash. Nan!

Sir Abel. Blockhead! The ploughing match shall take place as soon as Sir Philip Blandford and his daughter arrive.

Ash. Oh, likely, likely.

Enter Servant

Serv. Sir Abel, I beg to say, my master will be here immediately.

Sir Abel. And, sir, I beg to ask who possesses the happiness of being your master?

Serv. Your son, sir, Mr. Robert Handy.

Sir Abel. Indeed! and where is Bob?

Serv. I left him, sir, in the belfrey of the church.

Sir Abel. Where?

Serv. In the belfrey of the church.

Sir Abel. In the belfrey of the church! What was he doing there?

Serv. Why, Sir, the *natives* were ringing a peal in honour of our arrival–when my master finding they knew nothing of the matter, went up to the steeple to instruct them, and ordered me to proceed to the Castle–Give me leave, Sir Abel, to take this out of your way. [*Takes the camp chair.*] Sir, I have the honour–

[*Bows and Exit.*

Sir Abel. Wonderful! My Bob, you must know, is an astonishing fellow!–you have heard of the *admirable Crichton,* may be? Bob's of the same kidney! I contrive, he executes–Sir Abel *invenit,* Bob *fecit.* He can do everything–everything!

Ash. All the better vor he. I zay, zur, as he can turn his head to everything, pray, in what way med he earn his livelihood?

Sir Abel. Earn his livelihood!

Ash. Ees, zur;–How do he gain his bread!

Sir Abel. Bread! Oh, he can't earn his bread, bless you! he's a genius.

Ash. Genius! Drabbit it, I have got a horze o' thic name, but dom' un, he'll never work–never.

Sir Abel. Egad; here comes my boy Bob!–Eh! no–it is not! no.

Enter POSTBOY, *with a round hat and cane.*

Why, who the devil are you?

Postb. I am the postboy, your honour, but the gem'man said I did not know how to drive, so he mounted my horse, and made me get inside–Here he is.

Enter Handy

, jun. *with a postboy's cap and whip.*

Handy, jun. Ah, my old Dad, is that you?

Sir Abel. Certainly! the only doubt is, if that be you?

Handy, jun. Oh, I was teaching this fellow to drive–Nothing is so horrible as people pretending to do what they are unequal to–Give me my hat–That's the way to use a whip.

Postb. Sir, you know you have broke the horses' knees all to pieces.

Handy, jun. Hush, there's a guinea.

[*Apart.*

Sir Abel. [*To* Ashfield

.] You see, Bob can do everything. But, sir, when you knew I had arrived from Germany, why did you not pay your duty to me in London?

Handy, jun. Sir, I heard you were but four days married, and I would not interrupt your honeymoon.

Sir Abel. Four days! oh, you might have come.

[*Sighing.*

Handy, jun. I hear you have taken to your arms a simple rustic, unsophisticated by fashionable follies–a full blown blossom of nature.

Sir Abel. Yes!

Handy, jun. How does it answer?

Sir Abel. So, so!

Handy, jun. Any thorns?

Sir Abel. A few.

Handy, jun. I must be introduced–where is she?

Sir Abel. Not within thirty miles; for I don't hear her.

Ash. Ha, ha, ha!

Handy, jun. Who is that?

Sir Abel. Oh, a pretty behaved tittering friend of mine.

Ash. Zarvent, zur–No offence, I do hope–Could not help tittering a bit at Nelly–when she were zarvent maid wi' I, she had a tightish prattle wi' her, that's vor zartain.

Handy, jun. Oh! so then my honoured mamma was the servant of this tittering gentleman–I say, father, perhaps she has not lost the tightish prattle he speaks of.

Sir Abel. My dear boy, come here–Prattle! I say did you ever live next door to a pewterer's?–that's all–you understand me–did you ever hear a dozen fire-engines full gallop?–were you ever at Billingsgate in the sprat season?–or——

Handy, jun. Ha, ha!

Sir Abel. Nay, don't laugh, Bob.

Handy, jun. Indeed, sir, you think of it too seriously. The storm, I dare say, soon blows over.

Sir Abel. Soon! you know what a trade wind is, don't you, Bob? why, she thinks no more of the latter end of her speech, than she does of the latter end of her life–

Handy, jun. Ha! ha!

Sir Abel. But I won't be laugh'd at–I'll knock any man down that laughs! Bob, if you can say any thing pleasant, I'll trouble you; if not, do what my wife can't–hold your tongue.

Handy, jun. I'll shew you what I can do–I'll amuse you with this native.
[*Apart.*

Sir Abel. Do–do–quiz him–at him, Bob.

Handy, jun. I say, Farmer, you are a set of jolly fellows here, an't you?

Ash. Ees, zur, deadly jolly–excepting when we be otherwise, and then we bean't.

Handy, jun. Play at cricket, don't you?

Ash. Ees, zur; we Hampshire lads conceat we can bowl a bit or thereabouts.

Handy, jun. And cudgel too, I suppose?

Sir Abel. At him, Bob.

Ash. Ees, zur, we sometimes break oon another's heads, by way of being agreeable, and the like o'that.

Handy, jun. Understand all the guards? [*Putting himself in an attitude of cudgelling.*]

Ash. Can't zay I do, zur.

Handy, jun. What! hit in this way, eh? [*Makes a hit at* Ashfield
, *which he parries, and hits young* Handy
violently.]

Ash. Noa, zur, we do hit thic way.

Handy, jun. Zounds and fury!

Sir Abel. Why, Bob, he has broke your head.

Handy, jun. Yes; he rather hit me–he somehow—-

Sir Abel. He did indeed, Bob.

Handy, jun. Damn him–The fact is, I am out of practice.

Ash. You need not be, zur; I'll gi' ye a belly full any day, wi' all my heart and soul.

Handy, jun. No, no, thank you–Farmer, what's your name?

Ash. My name be Tummas Ashfield–any thing to say against my name?

[*Threatening.*

Handy, jun. No, no–Ashfield! shou'd he be the father of my pretty Susan–Pray have you a daughter?

Ash. Ees, I have–any thing to zay against she?

Handy, jun. No, no; I think her a charming creature.

Ash. Do ye, faith and troth–Come, that be deadly kind o'ye however–Do you zee, I were *frightful* she were not agreeable.

Handy, jun. Oh, she's extremely agreeable to me, I assure you.

Ash. I vow, it be quite pratty in you to take notice of Sue. I do hope, zur, breaking your head will break noa squares–She be a coming down to theas parts wi' lady our maid Nelly, as wur–your spouse, zur.

Handy, jun. The devil she is! that's awkward!

Ash. I do hope you'll be kind to Sue when she do come, woolye, zur?

Handy, jun. You may depend on it.

Sir Abel. I dare say you may. Come, Farmer, attend us.

Ash. Ees, zur; wi' all respect–Gentlemen, pray walk thic way, and I'll walk before you.

[*Exit.*

Sir Abel. Now, that's what he calls behaving pretty. Damn his pretty behaviour.

[*Exeunt.*

SCENE III.

A Grove.

[Morrington

comes down the stage, wrapped in a great coat–He looks about–then at his watch, and whistles–which is answered.]

Enter Gerald

.

Mor. Here, Gerald! Well, my trusty fellow, is Sir Philip arrived?

Ger. No, sir; but hourly expected.

Mor. Tell me, how does the castle look?

Ger. Sadly decayed, sir.

Mor. I hope, Gerald, you were not observed.

Ger. I fear otherwise, sir; on the skirts of the domain I encountered a stripling with his gun; but I darted into that thicket, and so avoided him.

[Henry

appears in the back ground, in a shooting dress, attentively observing them.]

Mor. Have you gained any intelligence?

Ger. None: the report that reached us was false–The infant certainly died with its mother–Hush! conceal yourself–we are observed–this way.

[*They retreat*–Henry
advances.

Henry. Hold! as a friend, one word!

[*They exeunt, he follows them, and returns.*

Again they have escaped me–"*The infant died with its mother*"–This agony of doubt
is insupportable.

Enter Evergreen

.

Everg. Henry, well met.

Henry. Have you seen strangers?

Everg. No!

Henry. Two but now have left this place–They spoke of a lost child–My busy fancy
led me to think I was the object of their search–I pressed forward, but they avoided
me.

Everg. No, no; it could not be you; for no one on earth knows but myself, and—-

Henry. Who? Sir Philip Blandford?

Everg. I am sworn, you know, my dear boy; I am solemnly sworn to silence.

Henry. True, my good old friend; and if the knowledge of who I am can only be
obtained at the price of thy perjury, let me for ever remain ignorant–let the corroding
thought still haunt my pillow, cross me at every turn, and render me insensible to the
blessings of health and liberty–yet, in vain do I suppress the thought–who am I? why
thus abandoned? perhaps the despised offspring of guilt–Ah! is it so?

[*Seizing him violently.*

Everg. Henry, do I deserve this?

Henry. Pardon me, good old man! I'll act more reasonably–I'll deem thy silence
mercy.

Everg. That's wisely said.

Henry. Yet it is hard to think, that the most detested reptile that nature forms, or
man pursues, has, when he gains his den, a parent's pitying breast to shelter in; but
I—-

Everg. Come, come, no more of this.

Henry. Well!—-I visited to-day that young man who was so grievously bruised by
the breaking of his team.

Everg. That was kindly done, Henry.

Henry. I found him suffering under extreme torture, yet a ray of joy shot from his
languid eye–for his medicine was administered by a father's hand–it was a mother's
precious tear that dropped upon his wound–Oh, how I envied him!

Everg. Still on the same subject–I tell thee, if thou art not acknowledged by thy
race, why, then become the noble founder of a new one.–Come with me to the castle,
for the last time.

Henry. The last time!

Everg. Aye, boy; for, when Sir Philip arrives, you must avoid him.

Henry. Not see him! where exists the power that shall prevent me?

Everg. Henry, if you value your own peace of mind–if you value an old man's
comfort, avoid the castle.

Henry. [*Aside.*] I must dissemble with this honest creature–Well, I am content.

Everg. That's right–that's right,–Henry–Be but thou resigned and virtuous, and He, who clothes the lily of the field, will be a parent to thee.

[*Exeunt.*

ACT THE SECOND.

SCENE I.

A Lodge belonging to the Castle.

Dame Ashfield discovered making lace.

Enter Handy

, *jun.*

Handy, jun. A singular situation this my old dad has placed me in; brought me here to marry a woman of fashion and beauty, while I have been professing, and I've a notion feeling, the most ardent love for the pretty Susan Ashfield–Propriety says, take Miss Blandford–Love says, take Susan–Fashion says, take both–but would Susan consent to such an arrangement?–and if she refused, would I consent to part with her?–Oh, time enough to put that question, when the previous one is disposed of–[*Seeing* Dame

.] How do you do? How do you do?–Making lace, I perceive–Is it a common employment, here?

Dame. Oh, no, sir? nobody can make it in these parts but myself!–Mrs. Grundy, indeed, pretends–but, poor woman! she knows no more of it than you do.

Handy, jun. Than I do! that's vastly well;–My dear madam, I passed two months at Mechlin for the express purpose.

Dame. Indeed!

Handy, jun. You don't do it right–now I can do it much better than that. Give me leave, and I'll shew you the true Mechlin method [*Turns the cushion round, kneels down, and begins working.*] First you see, so–then, so–

Enter Sir Abel

, *and* Miss Blandford

.

Sir Abel. I vow, Miss Blandford, fair as I ever thought you, the air of your native land has given additional lustre to your charms!–[*Aside.*] If my wife looked so–Ah! but where can Bob be?–You must know, miss, my son is a very clever fellow! you won't find him wasting his time in boyish frivolity!–no; you will find him–

[*Sees him.*

Miss B. Is that your son, sir?

Sir Abel. [*Abashed.*] Yes, that's Bob!

Miss B. Pray, sir, is he making lace, or is he making love?

Sir Abel. Curse me if I can tell. [*Hits him with his stick.*] Get up, you dog! don't you see Miss Blandford?

Handy, jun. [*Starting up.*] Zounds! how unlucky! Ma'am, your most obedient servant. [*Endeavours to hide the work.*] Curse the cushion!

[*Throws it off.*

Dame. Oh! he has spoiled my lace!

Handy, jun. Hush! I'll make you a thousand yards another time–You see, ma'am, I was explaining to this good woman–what–what need not be explained again–Admirably handsome, by Heaven!

[*Aside.*

Sir Abel. Is not she, Bob?

Handy, jun. [*To* Miss B

.] In your journey from the coast, I conclude you took London in your way? Hush!

[*To* Dame

.

Miss B. Oh no, sir, I could not so soon venture into the *beau monde*; a stranger just arrived from Germany–

Handy, jun. The very reason–the most fashionable introduction possible! but I perceive, sir, you have here imitated other German importations, and only restored to us our native excellence.

Miss B. I assure you, sir, I am eager to seize my birthright, the pure and envied immunities of an English woman!

Handy, jun. Then I trust, madam, you will be patriot enough to agree with me, that as a nation is poor, whose only wealth is importation–that therefore the humble native artist may ever hope to obtain from his countrymen those fostering smiles, without which genius must sicken and industry decay. But it requires no *valet de place* to conduct you through the purlieus of fashion, for now the way of the world is, for every one to pursue their own way; and following the fashion is differing as much as possible from the rest of your acquaintance.

Miss B. But, surely sir, there is some distinguishing feature, by which the votaries of fashion are known?

Handy, jun. Yes; but that varies extremely–sometimes fashionable celebrity depends on a high waist–sometimes on a low carriage–sometimes on high play, and sometimes on low breeding–last winter it rested solely on green peas!

Miss B. Green peas!

Handy, jun. Green peas–That lady was the most enchanting, who could bring the greatest quantity of green peas to her table at Christmas! the struggle was tremendous! Mrs. Rowley Powley had the best of it by five pecks and a half, but it having been unfortunately proved, that at her ball there was room to dance and eat conveniently–that no lady received a black eye, and no coachman was killed, the thing was voted decent and comfortable, and scouted accordingly.

Miss B. Is comfort then incompatible with fashion?

Handy, jun. Certainly!–Comfort in high life would be as preposterous as a lawyer's bag crammed with truth, or his wig decorated with coquelicot ribbons! No–it is not comfort and selection that is sought, but numbers and confusion! So that a fashionable party resembles Smithfield market,–only a good one when plentifully stocked–and ladies are reckoned by the score, like sheep, and their husbands by droves, like horned cattle!

Miss B. Ha, ha! and the conversation–

Handy, jun. Oh! like the assembly–confused, vapid, and abundant; as "How do, ma'am!–no accident at the door?–he, he!"–"Only my carriage broke to pieces!"–"I hope you had not your pocket picked!"–"Won't you sit down to faro?"–"Have you many to-night?"–"A few, about six hundred!"–"Were you at Lady Overall's?"–"Oh yes; a delicious crowd, and plenty of peas, he, he!"–and thus runs the fashionable race.

Sir Abel. Yes; and a precious run it is–full gallop all the way: first they run on–then their fortune is run through–then bills are run up–then they are run hard–then they've a run of luck–then they run out, and then they run away!–But I'll forgive fashion all its follies in consideration of one of its blessed laws.

Handy, jun. What may that be!

Sir Abel. That husband and wife must never be seen together.

Enter Servant

Serv. Miss Blandford, your father expects you.

Miss B. I hope I shall find him more composed.

Handy, jun. Is Sir Philip ill?

Miss B. His spirits are extremely depressed, and since we arrived here this morning his dejection has dreadfully increased.

Handy, jun. But I hope we shall be able to laugh away despondency.

Miss B. Sir, if you are pleased to consider my esteem as an object worth your possession, I know no way of obtaining it so certain as by your shewing every attention to my dear father.

[*As they are going,*
Enter Ashfield

Ash. Dame! Dame! she be come!

Dame. Who? Susan! our dear Susan?

Ash. Ees–zo–come along–Oh, Sir Abel! Lady Nelly, your spouse, do order you to go to her directly!

Handy, jun. Order! you mistake–

Sir Abel. No, he don't–she generally prefers that word.

Miss B. Adieu! Sir Abel.

[*Exeunt* Miss Blandford
and Handy
, jun.

Sir Abel. Oh! if my wife had such a pretty way with her mouth.

Dame. And how does Susan look?

Ash. That's what I do want to know, zoa come along–Woo ye though–Missus, let's behave pratty–Zur if you pleaze, Dame and I will let you walk along wi' us.

Sir Abel. How condescending! Oh, you are a pretty behaved fellow!

[*Exeunt.*

SCENE II.

Farmer Ashfield's
Kitchen.

Enter Lady Handy
and Susan

Susan. My dear home, thrice welcome!–What gratitude I feel to your ladyship for this indulgence!

Lady H. That's right, child!

Susan. And I am sure you partake my pleasure in again visiting a place, where you received every protection and kindness my parents could shew you, for, I remember, while you lived with my father–

Lady H. Child! don't put your memory to any fatigue on my account–you may transfer the remembrance of who I was, to aid your more perfect recollection of who I am.

Susan. Lady Handy!

Lady H. That's right, child!–I am not angry.

Susan. [*Looking out.*] Ah! I see my dear father and mother coming through the garden.

Lady H. Oh! now I shall be caressed to death; but I must endure the shock of their attentions.

Enter Farmer
and Dame
, *with* Sir Abel

.

Ash. My dear Susan!

[*They run to* Susan

.

Dame. My sweet child! give me a kiss.

Ash. Hald thee! Feyther first though–Well, I be as mortal glad to zee thee as never war–and how be'st thee? and how do thee like Lunnun town? it be a deadly lively place I be tuold.

Dame. Is not she a sweet girl?

Sir Abel. That she is.

Lady H. [*With affected dignity.*] Does it occur to any one present, that Lady Handy is in the room?

Sir Abel. Oh, Lud! I'm sure, my dear wife, I never forget, that you are in the room.

Ash. Drabbitit! I overlooked Lady Nelly, sure enow; but consider, there be zome difference between thee and our own Susan! I be deadly glad to zee thee, however.

Dame. So am I, Lady Handy.

Ash. Don't ye take it unkind I han't a buss'd thee yet–meant no slight indeed.

[*Kisses her.*

Lady H. Oh! shocking!

[*Aside.*

Ash. No harm I do hope, zur.

Sir Abel. None at all.

Ash. But dash it, Lady Nelly, what do make thee paint thy vace all over we rud ochre zoo? Be it vor thy spouse to knaw thee?–that be the way I do knaw my sheep.

Sir Abel. The flocks of fashion are all marked so, Farmer.

Ash. Likely! Drabbit it! thee do make a tightish kind of a ladyship zure enow.

Dame. That you do, my lady! you remember the old house?

Ash. Aye; and all about it, doant ye? Nelly! my lady!

Lady H. Oh! I'm quite shock'd–Susan, child! prepare a room where I may dress before I proceed to the castle.

[*Exit* Susan

.

Enter Handy
, jun.

Handy, jun. I don't see Susan–I say, Dad, is that my mamma?

Sir Abel. Yes–speak to her.

Handy, jun. [*Chucking her under the chin*] A fine girl, upon my soul!

Lady H. Fine girl, indeed! Is this behaviour!

Handy, jun. Oh! beg pardon, most honoured parent. [*She curtsies.*]—that's a damned bad curtsey, I can teach you to make a much better curtsey than that!

Lady H. You teach me, that am old enough to–hem!

Handy, jun. Oh! that toss of the head was very bad indeed–Look at me!–That's the thing!

Lady H. Am I to be insulted? Sir Abel, you know I seldom condescend to talk.

Sir Abel. Don't say so, my lady, you wrong yourself.

Lady H. But, when I do begin, you know not where it will end.

Sir Abel. Indeed I do not.

[*Aside.*

Lady H. I insist on receiving all possible respect from your son.

Handy, jun. And you shall have it, my dear girl!–Madam, I mean.

Lady H. I vow, I am agitated to that degree–Sir Abel! my fan.

Sir Abel. Yes, my dear–Bob, look here, a little contrivance of my own. While others carry swords and such like dreadful weapons in their canes, I more gallantly carry a fan. [*Removes the head of his cane, and draws out a fan.*] A pretty thought, isn't it? [*Presents it to his lady.*]

Ash. Some difference between thic stick and mine, beant there, zur?

[*To* Handy
, jun.

Handy, jun. [*Moving away.*] Yes, there is.–[*To Lady H.*] Do you call that fanning yourself? [*Taking the fan.*] My dear ma'am, this is the way to man uvre a fan.

Lady H. Sir, you shall find [*To* Handy
, jun.] I have power enough to make you repent this behaviour, severely repent it–Susan!

[*Exit followed by* Dame

.

Handy, jun. Bravo! passion becomes her; she does that vastly well.

Sir Abel. Yes, practice makes perfect.

Enter Susan

.

Susan. Did your ladyship call?–Heavens! Mr. Handy!

Handy, jun. Hush! my angel! be composed! that letter will explain. [*Giving a letter, noticed by* Ashfield
.] Lady Handy wishes to see you.
    Susan. Oh, Robert!
    Handy, jun. At present, my love, no more.
    [*Exit* Susan, *followed by* Ashfield

    Sir Abel. What were you saying, sir, to that young woman?
    Handy, jun. Nothing particular, sir. Where is Lady Handy going?
    Sir Abel. To dress.
    Handy, jun. I suppose she has found out the use of money.
    Sir Abel. Yes; I'll do her the justice to say she encourages trade.–Why, do you know, Bob, my best coal pit won't find her in white muslins–round her neck hangs an hundred acres at least; my noblest oaks have made wigs for her; my fat oxen have dwindled into Dutch pugs, and white mice; my India bonds are transmuted into shawls and otto of roses; and a magnificent mansion has shrunk into a diamond snuff-box.
    Enter Countryman

    Coun. Gentlemen, the folks be all got together, and the ploughs be ready–and——
    Sir Abel. We are coming.
    [*Exit* Servant

    Handy, jun. Ploughs?
    Sir Abel. Yes, Bob, we are going to have a grand agricultural meeting.
    Handy, jun. Indeed!
    Sir Abel. If I could but find a man able to manage my new-invented *curricle* plough, none of them would have a chance.
    Handy, jun. My dear sir, if there be any thing on earth I can do, it is that.
    Sir Abel. What!
    Handy. I rather fancy I can plough better than any man in England.
    Sir Abel. You don't say so! What a clever fellow he is! I say, Bob, if you would–
    Handy, jun. No! I can't condescend.
    Sir Abel. Condescend! why not?–much more creditable, let me tell you, than galloping a maggot for a thousand, or eating a live cat, or any other fashionable achievement.
    Handy, jun. So it is–Egad! I will–I'll carry off the prize of industry.
    Sir Abel. But should you lose, Bob.
    Handy, jun. I lose! that's vastly well!
    Sir Abel. True, with my curricle plough you could hardly fail.
    Handy, jun. With my superior skill, Dad–Then, I say, how the newspapers will teem with the account.
    Sir Abel. Yes.
    Handy, jun. That universal genius, Handy, junior, with a plough——
    Sir Abel. Stop–invented by that ingenious machinist, Handy, senior.

Handy, jun. Gained the prize against the first husbandmen in Hampshire–Let our Bond-street butterflies emulate the example of Handy, junior.–

Sir Abel. And let old city grubs cultivate the field of science, like Handy, senior– Ecod! I am so happy!

Lady H. [*Without.*] Sir Abel!

Sir Abel. Ah! there comes a damper.

Handy, jun. Courage! you have many resources of happiness.

Sir Abel. Have I? I should be very glad to know them.

Handy, jun. In the first place you possess an excellent temper.

Sir Abel. So much the worse; for if I had a bad one, I should be the better able to conquer hers.

Handy, jun. You enjoy good health–

Sir Abel. So much the worse; for if I were ill, she wouldn't come near me.

Handy, jun. Then you are rich–

Sir Abel. So much the worse; for had I been poor, she would not have married me. But I, say, Bob, if you gain the prize, I'll have a patent for my plough.

Lady H. [*Without.*] Sir Abel! I say–

Handy, jun. Father, could not you get a patent for stopping that sort of noise?

Sir Abel. If I could, what a sale it would have!–No, Bob, a patent has been obtained for the only thing that will silence her–

Handy, jun. Aye–What's that?

Sir Abel. [*In a whisper.*] A coffin! hush!–I'm coming, my dear.

Handy, jun. Ha, ha, ha!

[*Exeunt.*

SCENE III.

A Parlour in Ashfield's
House.

Enter Ashfield
and Wife.

Ash. I tell ye, I zee'd un gi' Susan a letter, an I dan't like it a bit.

Dame. Nor I: if shame should come to the poor child–I say, Tummas, what would Mrs. Grundy say then?

Ash. Dom Mrs. Grundy; what would my poor wold heart zay? but I be bound it be all innocence.

Enter Henry

.

Dame. Ah, Henry! we have not seen thee at home all day.

Ash. And I do zomehow fanzie things dan't go zo clever when thee'rt away from farm.

Henry. My mind has been greatly agitated.

Ash. Well, won't thee go and zee the ploughing match?

Henry. Tell me, will not those who obtain prizes be introduced to the Castle?

Ash. Ees, and feasted in the great hall.

Henry. My good friend, I wish to become a candidate.

Dame. You, Henry!

Henry. It is time I exerted the faculties Heaven has bestowed on me; and though my heavy fate crushes the proud hopes this heart conceives, still let me prove myself worthy of the place Providence has assigned me.–[*Aside.*] Should I succeed, it will bring me to the presence of that man, who (I know not why) seems the dictator of my fate.–[*To them.*] Will you furnish me with the means?

Ash. Will I!–Thou shalt ha' the best plough in the parish–I wish it were all gould for thy zake–and better cattle there can't be noowhere.

Henry. Thanks, my good friend–my benefactor–I have little time for preparation– So receive my gratitude, and farewell.

[*Exit.*

Dame. A blessing go with thee!

Ash. I zay, Henry, take Jolly, and Smiler, and Captain, but dan't ye take thic lazy beast Genius–I'll be shot if having vive load an acre on my wheat land could please me more.

Dame. Tummas, here comes Susan reading the letter.

Ash. How pale she do look! dan't she?

Dame. Ah! poor thing!–If——

Ash. Hauld thy tongue, woolye?

[*They retire.*

Enter Susan
, *reading the letter.*

Susan. Is it possible! Can the man to whom I've given my heart write thus!–"I am compelled to marry Miss Blandford; but my love for my Susan is unalterable– I hope she will not, for an act of necessity, cease to think with tenderness on her faithful Robert."——Oh man! ungrateful man! it is from our bosoms alone you derive your power; how cruel then to use it, in fixing in those bosoms endless sorrow and despair!——"Still think with tenderness"–Base, dishonourable insinuation–He might have allowed me to esteem him. [*Locks up the letter in a box on the table, and exit weeping.*]

[Ashfield
and Dame
come forward.]

Ash. Poor thing!–What can be the matter–She locked up the letter in thic box, and then burst into tears.

[*Looks at the box.*

Dame. Yes, Tummas; she locked it in that box sure enough.

[*Shakes a bunch of keys that hangs at her side.*

Ash. What be doing, Dame? what be doing?

Dame. [*With affected indifference.*] Nothing; I was only touching these keys.

[*They look at the box and keys significantly.*

Ash. A good tightish bunch!

Dame. Yes; they are of all sizes.

[*They look as before.*

Ash. Indeed!–Well–Eh!–Dame, why dan't ye speak? thou canst chatter fast enow zometimes.

Dame. Nay, Tummas–I dare say–if–you know best–but I think I could find—-

Ash. Well, Eh!–you can just try you knaw [*Greatly agitated.*] You can try, just vor the vun on't: but mind, dan't ye make a noise. [*She opens it.*] Why, thee hasn't opened it?

Dame. Nay, Tummas! you told me!

Ash. Did I?

Dame. There's the letter!

Ash. Well, why do ye gi't to I?–I dan't want it, I'm sure. [*Taking it–he turns it over–she eyes it eagerly–he is about to open it.*]–She's coming! she's coming! [*He conceals the letter, they tremble violently.*] No, she's gone into t'other room. [*They hang their heads dejectedly, then look at each other.*] What mun that feyther an mother be doing, that do blush and tremble at their own dater's coming. [*Weeps.*] Dang it, has she desarv'd it of us–Did she ever deceive us?–Were she not always the most open hearted, dutifullest, kindest–and thee to goa like a dom'd spy, and open her box, poor thing!

Dame. Nay, Tummas—-

Ash. You did–I zaw you do it myzel!–you look like a thief, now–you doe–Hush!– no–Dame–here be the letter–I won't reead a word on't; put it where thee vound it, and as thee vound it.

Dame. With all my heart.

[*She returns the letter to the box.*]

Ash. [*Embraces her.*] Now I can wi' pleasure hug my wold wife, and look my child in the vace again–I'll call her, and ax her about it; and if she dan't speak without disguisement, I'll be bound to be shot–Dame, be the colour of sheame off my face yet?–I never zeed thee look ugly before——Susan, my dear Sue, come here a bit, woollye?

Enter Susan

.

Susan. Yes, my dear father.

Ash. Sue, we do wish to give thee a bit of admonishing and parent-like conzultation.

Susan. I hope I have ever attended to your admonitions.

Ash. Ees, bless thee, I do believe thee hast, lamb; but we all want our memories jogg'd a bit, or why else do parson preach us all to sleep every Zunday–Zo thic be the topic–Dame and I, Sue, did zee a lctter gi'd to thee, and thee–bursted into tears, and lock'd un up in thic box–and then Dame and I–we–that's all.

Susan. My dear father, if I concealed the contents of that letter from your knowl- edge, it was because I did not wish your heart to share in the pain mine feels.

Ash. Dang it, didn't I tell thee zoo?

[*To his wife.*

Dame. Nay, Tummas, did I say otherwise?

Susan. Believe me, my dear parents, my heart never gave birth to a thought my tongue feared to utter.

Ash. There, the very words I zaid?

Susan. If you wish to see the letter, I will shew it to you.

[*She searches for the key.*

Dame. Here's a key will open it.

Ash. Drabbit it, hold thy tongue, thou wold fool? [*Aside.*] No, Susan. I'll not zee it–I'll believe my child.

Susan. You shall not find your confidence ill-placed–it is true the gentleman declared he loved me; it is equally true that declaration was not unpleasing to me– Alas! it is also true, that his letter contains sentiments disgraceful to himself, and insulting to me.

Ash. Drabbit it, if I'd knaw'd that, when we were cudgelling a bit, I wou'd ha' lapt my stick about his ribs pratty tightish, I wou'd.

Susan. Pray, father, don't you resent his conduct to me.

Ash. What! mayn't I lather un a bit?

Susan. Oh, no! I've the strongest reasons to the contrary!

Ash. Well, Sue, I won't–I'll behave as pratty as I always do–but it be time to go to the green, and zee the fine zights–How I do hate the noise of thic dom'd bunch of keys–But bless thee, my child–dan't forget that vartue to a young woman be vor all the world like–like–Dang it, I ha' gotten it all in my head; but zomehow–I can't talk it–but vartue be to a young woman what corn be to a blade o'wheat, do you zee; for while the corn be there it be glorious to the eye, and it be called the staff of life; but take that treasure away, and what do remain? why nought but thic worthless straw that man and beast do tread upon.

[*Exeunt.*

SCENE IV.

An extensive view of a cultivated country–A ploughed field in the centre, in which are seen six different ploughs and horses–At one side a handsome tent–A number of country people assembled.

Enter Ashfield

and Dame

.

Ash. Make way, make way for the gentry! and, do ye hear, behave pratty as I do–Dang thee, stond back, or I'll knack thee down, I wool.

Enter Sir Abel

, *and* Miss Blandford

, *with Servants.*

Sir Abel. It is very kind of you to honour our rustic festivities with your presence.

Miss B. Pray, Sir Abel, where is your son?

Sir Abel. What! Bob? Oh, you'll see him presently–[*Nodding significantly.*]–Here are the prize medals; and if you will condescend to present them, I'm sure they'll be worn with additional pleasure.–I say, you'll see Bob presently.–Well, Farmer, is it all over?

Ash. Ees, zur; the acres be plough'd and the ground judg'd; and the young lads be coming down to receive their reward–Heartily welcome, miss, to your native land; hope you be as pleased to zee we as we be to zee you, and the like o'that.–Mortal beautizome to be sure–I declare, miss, it do make I quite warm zomehow to look at ye. [*A shout without.*] They be coming–Now, Henry!

Sir Abel. Now you'll see Bob!–now my dear boy, Bob!–here he comes.

[*Huzza.*

Enter Henry

and two young Husbandmen.

Ash. 'Tis he, he has don't–Dang you all, why dan't ye shout? Huzza!

Sir Abel. Why, zounds, where's Bob?–I don't see Bob–Bless me, what has become of Bob and my plough?

[*Retires and takes out his glass.*

Ash. Well, Henry, there be the prize, and there be the fine lady that will gi' it thee.

Henry. Tell me who is that lovely creature?

Ash. The dater of Sir Philip Blandford.

Henry. What exquisite sweetness! Ah! should the father but resemble her, I shall have but little to fear from his severity.

Ash. Miss, thic be the young man that ha got'n the goulden prize.

Miss B. This! I always thought ploughmen were coarse, vulgar creatures, but he seems handsome and diffident.

Ash. Ees, quite pratty behaved–it were I that teach'd un.

Miss B. What's your name?

Henry. Henry.

Miss B. And your family?

[Henry

, in agony of grief, turns away, strikes his forehead, and leans on the shoulder of Ashfield

.]

Dame. [*Apart to* Miss B

.] Madam, I beg pardon, but nobody knows about his parentage; and when it is mentioned, poor boy! he takes on sadly–He has lived at our house ever since we had the farm, and we have had an allowance for him–small enough to be sure–but, good lad! he was always welcome to share what we had.

Miss B. I am shock'd at my imprudence–[*To* Henry

.] Pray pardon me; I would not insult an enemy, much less one I am inclined to admire–[*Giving her hand, then withdraws it.*]–to esteem–you shall go to the Castle–my father shall protect you.

Henry. Generous creature! to merit his esteem is the fondest wish of my heart–to be your slave, the proudest aim of my ambition.

Miss B. Receive your merited reward. [*He kneels–she places the medal round his neck–the same to the others.*]

Sir Abel. [*Advances.*] I can't see Bob: pray, sir, do you happen to know what is become of my Bob?

Henry. Sir?

Sir Abel. Did not you see a remarkable clever plough, and a young man——

Henry. At the beginning of the contest I observed a gentleman; his horses, I believe, were unruly; but my attention was too much occupied to allow me to notice more.

[*Laughing without.*

Handy, jun. [*Without.*] How dare you laugh?

Sir Abel. That's Bob's voice!

[*Laughing again.*

Enter Handy

, jun. *in a smock frock, cocked hat, and a piece of a plough in his hand.*

Handy, jun. Dare to laugh again, and I'll knock you down with this!–Ugh! how infernally hot!

[*Walks about.*

Sir Abel. Why, Bob, where have you been?

Handy, jun. I don't know where I've been.

Sir Abel. And what have you got in your hand?

Handy, jun. What! All I could keep of your nonsensical ricketty plough.

[*Walks about,* Sir Abel

following.

Sir Abel. Come, none of that, sir.–Don't abuse my plough, to cover your ignorance, sir? where is it, sir? and where are my famous Leicestershire horses, sir?

Handy, jun. Where? ha, ha, ha! I'll tell you as nearly as I can, ha, ha! What's the name of the next county?

Ash. It be called Wiltshire, zur.

Handy, jun. Then, dad, upon the nicest calculation I am able to make, they are at this moment engaged in the very patriotic act of ploughing Salisbury plain, ha ha! I saw them fairly over that hill, full gallop, with the curricle plough at their heels.

Ash. Ha, ha! a good one, ha ha!

Handy, jun. But never mind, father, you must again set your invention to work, and I my toilet:–rather a deranged figure to appear before a lady in. [*Fiddles.*] Hey day! What! are you going to dance?

Ash. Ees, zur; I suppose you can sheake a leg a bit?

Handy, jun. I fancy I can dance every possible step, from the *pas ruse* to the war-dance of the Catawbaws.

Ash. Likely.–I do hope, miss, you'll join your honest neighbours; they'll be deadly hurt an' you won't gig it a bit wi' un.

Miss B. With all my heart.

Sir Abel. Bob's an excellent dancer.

Miss B. I dare say he is, sir? but on this occasion, I think I ought to dance with the young man, who gained the prize–I think it would be most pleasant–most proper, I mean; and I am glad you agree with me.–So, sir, if you'll accept my hand–

[Henry

takes it.

Sir Abel. Very pleasantly settled, upon my soul!–Bob, won't you dance?

Handy, jun. I dance!–no, I'll look at them–I'll quietly look on.

Sir Abel. Egad now, as my wife's away, I'll try to find a pretty girl, and make one among them.

Ash. That's hearty!–Come, Dame, hang the rheumatics!–Now, lads and lasses, behave pratty, and strike up.

[*A dance.*

[Handy

, jun. *looks on a little, and then begins to move his legs–then dashes into the midst of the dance, and endeavours to imitate every one opposite to him; then being exhausted, he leaves the dance, seizes the fiddle, and plays 'till the curtain drops.*]

ACT THE THIRD.
SCENE I.
An Apartment in the Castle.

Sir Philip Blandford

discovered on a couch, reading, Servants *attending.*

Sir Philip. Is not my daughter yet returned?

Serv. No, Sir Philip.

Sir Philip. Dispatch a servant to her.

[*Exit* Servant

Re-enter Servant

Serv. Sir, the old gardener is below, and asks to see you.

Sir Philip. [*Rises and throws away the book.*] Admit him instantly, and leave me.–

[*Exit* Servant

Enter Evergreen

, who bows, then looking at Sir Philip

, clasps his hands together, and weeps.

Does this desolation affect the old man?–Come near me–Time has laid a lenient hand on thee.

Everg. Oh, my dear master! can twenty years have wrought the change I see?

Sir Philip. No; [*Striking his breast.*] 'tis the canker here that hath withered up my trunk;–but are we secure from observation?

Everg. Yes.

Sir Philip. Then tell me, does the boy live?

Everg. He does, and is as fine a youth–

Sir Philip. No comments.

Everg. We named him–

Sir Philip. Be dumb! let me not hear his name. Has care been taken he may not blast me with his presence?

Everg. It has, and he cheerfully complied.

Sir Philip. Enough! never speak of him more. Have you removed every dreadful vestige from the fatal chamber? [Evergreen *hesitates.*]–O speak!

Everg. My dear master! I confess my want of duty. Alas! I had not courage to go there.

Sir Philip. Ah!

Everg. Nay, forgive me! wiser than I have felt such terrors.–The apartments have been carefully locked up; the keys not a moment from my possession:–here they are.

Sir Philip. Then the task remains with me. Dreadful thought! I can well pardon thy fears, old man.–O! could I wipe from my memory that hour, when–

Everg. Hush! your daughter.

Sir Philip. Leave me—we'll speak anon.

[*Exit* Evergreen

Enter Miss Blandford

Miss B. Dear father! I came the moment I heard you wished to see me.

Sir Philip. My good child, thou art the sole support that props my feeble life. I fear my wish for thy company deprives thee of much pleasure.

Miss B. Oh no! what pleasure can be equal to that of giving you happiness? Am I not rewarded in seeing your eyes beam with pleasure on me?

Sir Philip. 'Tis the pale reflection of the lustre I see sparkling there.—But, tell me, did your lover gain the prize?

Miss B. Yes, papa.

Sir Philip. Few men of his rank—

Miss B. Oh! you mean Mr. Handy?

Sir Philip. Yes.

Miss B. No; he did not.

Sir Philip. Then, whom did *you* mean?

Miss B. Did you say lover? I–I mistook.–No–a young man called Henry obtained the prize.

Sir Philip. And how did Mr. Handy succeed?

Miss B. Oh! It was so ridiculous!–I will tell you, papa, what happened to him.

Sir Philip. To Mr. Handy?

Miss B. Yes; as soon as the contest was over Henry presented himself. I was surprised at seeing a young man so handsome and elegant as Henry is.–Then I placed the medal round Henry's neck, and was told, that poor Henry—

Sir Philip. Henry!–So, my love, this is your account of Mr. Robert Handy!

Miss B. Yes, papa–no, papa–he came afterwards, dressed so ridiculously, that even Henry could not help smiling.

Sir Philip. Henry again!

Miss B. Then we had a dance.

Sir Philip. Of course you danced with your lover?

Miss B. Yes, papa.

Sir Philip. How does Mr. Handy dance?

Miss B. Oh! he did not dance till—

Sir Philip. You danced with your lover?

Miss B. Yes–no papa!–Somebody said (I don't know who) that I ought to dance with Henry, because—

Sir Philip. Still Henry! Oh! some rustic boy. My dear child, you talk as if you loved this Henry.

Miss B. Oh! no, papa–and I am certain he don't love me.

Sir Philip. Indeed!

Miss B. Yes, papa; for, when he touched my hand, he trembled as if I terrified him; and instead of looking at me as you do, who I am sure love me, when our eyes met, he withdrew his and cast them on the ground.

Sir Philip. And these are the reasons, which make you conclude he does not love you?

Miss B. Yes, papa.

Sir Philip. And probably you could adduce proof equally convincing that you don't love him?

Miss B. Oh, yes–quite; for in the dance he sometimes paid attention to other young women, and I was so angry with him! Now, you know, papa, I love you–and I am sure I should not have been angry with you had you done so.

Sir Philip. But one question more–Do you think Mr. Handy loves you?

Miss B. I have never thought about it, papa.

Sir Philip. I am satisfied.

Miss B. Yes, I knew I should convince you.

Sir Philip. Oh, love; malign and subtle tyrant, how falsely art thou painted blind! 'tis thy votaries are so; for what but blindness can prevent their seeing thy poisoned shaft, which is for ever doomed to rankle in the victim's heart.

Miss B. Oh! now I am certain I am not in love; for I feel no rankling at my heart. I feel the softest, sweetest sensation I ever experienced. But, papa, you must come to the lawn. I don't know why, but to-day nature seems enchanting; the birds sing more sweetly, and the flowers give more perfume.

Sir Philip. [*Aside.*] Such was the day my youthful fancy pictured!–How did it close!

Miss B. I promised Henry your protection.

Sir Philip. Indeed! that was much. Well I will see your rustic here. This infant passion must be crushed. Poor wench! some artless boy has caught thy youthful fancy.–Thy arm, my child.

[*Exeunt.*

SCENE II.

A Lawn before the Castle.

Enter Henry

and Ashfield

.

Ash. Well! here thee'rt going to make thy bow to Sir Philip. I zay, if he should take a fancy to thee, thou'lt come to farm, and zee us zometimes, wo'tn't, Henry?

Henry. [*Shaking his hand.*] Tell me, is that Sir Philip Blandford, who leans on that lady's arm?

Ash. I don't know, by reason, d'ye zee, I never zeed'un. Well, good bye! I declare thee doz look quite grand with thic golden prize about thy neck, vor all the world like the lords in their stars, that do come to theas pearts to pickle their skins in the zalt zea ocean! Good b'ye, Henry!

[*Exit.*

Henry. He approaches! why this agitation? I wish, yet dread, to meet him.

Enter Sir Philip
and Miss Blandford
, attended.

Miss B. The joy your tenantry display at seeing you again must be truly grateful to you.

Sir Philip. No, my child; for I feel I do not merit it. Alas! I can see no orphans clothed with my beneficence, no anguish assuaged by my care.

Miss B. Then I am sure my dear father wishes to show his kind intentions. So I will begin by placing one under his protection [*Goes up the stage, and leads down* Henry . Sir Philip
, on seeing him, starts, then becomes greatly agitated.]

Sir Philip. Ah! do my eyes deceive me! No, it must be him! Such was the face his father wore.

Henry. Spake you of my father?

Sir Philip. His presence brings back recollections, which drive me to madness!–How came he here?–Who have I to curse for this?

Miss B. [*Falling on his neck.*] Your daughter.

Henry. Oh sir! tell me–on my knees I ask it! do my parents live! Bless me with my father's name, and my days shall pass in active gratitude–my nights in prayers for you. [Sir Philip
views him with severe contempt.] Do not mock my misery! Have you a heart?

Sir Philip. Yes; of marble. Cold and obdurate to the world–ponderous and painful to myself–Quit my sight for ever!

Miss B. Go, Henry, and save me from my father's curse.

Henry. I obey: cruel as the command is, I obey it–I shall often look at this, [*Touching the medal.*] and think on the blissful moment, when your hand placed it there.

Sir Philip. Ah! tear it from his breast.
[Servant
advances.

Henry. Sooner take my life! It is the first honour I have earned, and it is no mean one; for it assigns me the first rank among the sons of industry! This is my claim to the sweet rewards of honest labour! This will give me competence, nay more, enable me to despise your tyranny!

Sir Philip. Rash boy, mark! Avoid me, and be secure.–Repeat this intrusion, and my vengeance shall pursue thee.

Henry. I defy its power!–You are in England, sir, where the man, who bears about him an upright heart, bears a charm too potent for tyranny to humble. Can your frown wither up my youthful vigour? No!–Can your malediction disturb the slumbers of a quiet conscience? No! Can your breath stifle in my heart the adoration it feels for that pitying angel? Oh, no!

Sir Philip. Wretch! you shall be taught the difference between us!

Henry. I feel it now! proudly feel it!–You hate the man, that never wronged you–I could love the man, that injures me–You meanly triumph o'er a worm–I make a giant tremble.

Sir Philip. Take him from my sight! Why am I not obeyed?

Miss B. Henry, if you wish my hate should not accompany my father's, instantly begone.

Henry. Oh, pity me!

[*Exit.*

[Miss Blandford

looks after him–Sir Philip

, *exhausted, leans on his servants.*

Sir Philip. Supported by my servants! I thought I had a daughter!

Miss B. [*Running to him.*] O you have, my father! one that loves you better than her life!

Sir Philip. [*To* Servant

.] Leave us. [*Exit* Servant

. Emma, if you feel, as I fear you do, love for that youth–mark my words! When the dove wooes for its mate the ravenous kite; when nature's fixed antipathies mingle in sweet concord, then, and not till then, hope to be united.

Miss B. O Heaven!

Sir Philip. Have you not promised me the disposal of your hand?

Miss B. Alas! my father! I didn't then know the difficulty of obedience!

Sir Philip. Hear, then, the reasons why I demand compliance. You think I hold these rich estates–Alas, the shadow only, not the substance.

Miss B. Explain, my father!

Sir Philip. When I left my native country, I left it with a heart lacerated by every wound, that the falsehood of others, or my own conscience, could inflict. Hateful to myself, I became the victim of dissipation–I rushed to the gaming table, and soon became the dupe of villains.–My ample fortune was lost; I detected one in the act of fraud, and having brought him to my feet, he confessed a plan had been laid for my ruin; that he was but an humble instrument; for that the man, who, by his superior genius, stood possessed of all the mortgages and securities I had given, was one Morrington.

Miss B. I have heard you name him before. Did you not know this Morrington?

Sir Philip. No; he, like his deeds, avoided the light–Ever dark, subtle, and mysterious. Collecting the scattered remnant of my fortune, I wandered, wretched and desolate, till, in a peaceful village, I first beheld thy mother, humble in birth, but exalted in virtue. The morning after our marriage she received a packet, containing these words: "The reward of virtuous love, presented by a repentant villain;" and which also contained bills and notes to the high amount of ten thousand pounds.

Miss B. And no name?

Sir Philip. None; nor could I ever guess at the generous donor. I need not tell thee what my heart suffered, when death deprived me of her. Thus circumstanced, this good man, Sir Abel Handy, proposed to unite our families by marriage; and in consideration of what he termed the honour of our alliance, agreed to pay off every incumbrance on my estates, and settle them as a portion on you and his son. Yet still another wonder remains.–When I arrive, I find no claim whatever has been made, either by Morrington or his agents. What am I to think? Can Morrington have perished, and with him his large claims to my property? Or, does he withhold the blow, to make it fall more heavily?

Miss B. 'Tis very strange! very mysterious! But my father has not told me what misfortune led him to leave his native country.

Sir Philip. [*Greatly agitated.*] Ha!

Miss B. May I not know it?

Sir Philip. Oh, never, never, never!

Miss B. I will not ask it–Be composed–Let me wipe away those drops of anguish from your brow.–How cold your cheek is! My father, the evening damps will harm you–Come in–I will be all you wish–indeed I will.

[*Exeunt.*

SCENE III.

An Apartment in the Castle.

Enter Evergreen

Everg. Was ever any thing so unlucky! Henry to come to the Castle and meet Sir Philip! He should have consulted me; I shall be blamed–but, thank Heaven, I am innocent.

[Sir Abel

and Lady Handy

without.]

Lady H. I will be treated with respect.

Sir Abel. You shall, my dear.

[*They enter.*

Lady H. But how! but how, Sir Abel? I repeat it–

Sir Philip. [*Aside.*] For the fiftieth time.

Lady H. Your son conducts himself with an insolence I won't endure; but you are ruled by him, you have no will of your own.

Sir Abel. I have not, indeed.

Lady H. How contemptible!

Sir Abel. Why, my dear, this is the case–I am like the ass in the fable; and if I am doomed to carry a packsaddle, it is not much matter who drives me.

Lady H. To yield your power to those the law allows you to govern!–

Sir Abel. Is very weak, indeed.

Everg. Lady Handy, your very humble servant; I heartily congratulate you, madam, on your marriage with this worthy gentleman–Sir, I give you joy.

Sir Abel. [*Aside.*] Not before 'tis wanted.

Everg. Aye, my lady, this match makes up for the imprudence of your first.

Lady H. Hem!

Sir Abel. Eh! What!–what's that–Eh! what do you mean?

Everg. I mean, sir–that Lady Handy's former husband–

Sir Abel. Former husband!–Why, my dear, I never knew–Eh!

Lady H. A mumbling old blockhead!–Didn't you, Sir Abel? Yes; I was rather married many years ago; but my husband went abroad and died.

Sir Abel. Died, did he?

Everg. Yes, sir, he was a servant in the Castle.

Sir Abel. Indeed! So he died–poor fellow!

Lady H. Yes.

Sir Abel. What, you are sure he died, are you?

Lady H. Don't you hear?

Sir Abel. Poor fellow! neglected perhaps–had I known it, he should have had the best advice money could have got.

Lady H. You seem sorry.

Sir Abel. Why, you would not have me pleased at the death of your husband, would you?–a good kind of man?

Everg. Yes; a faithful fellow–rather ruled his wife too severely.

Sir Abel. Did he! [*Apart to* Evergreen
.] Pray do you happen to recollect his manner!–Could you just give a hint of the way he had?

Lady H. Do you want to tyrannize over my poor tender heart?–'Tis too much!

Everg. Bless me! Lady Handy is ill–Salts! salts!

Sir Abel. [*Producing an essence box.*] Here are salts, or aromatic vinegar, or essence of–

Everg. Any–any.

Sir Abel. Bless me, I can't find the key!

Everg. Pick the lock.

Sir Abel. It can't be picked, it is a patent lock.

Everg. Then break it open, sir.

Sir Abel. It can't be broke open–it is a contrivance of my own–you see, here comes a horizontal bolt, which acts upon a spring, therefore–

Lady H. I may die, while you are describing a horizontal bolt. Do you think you shall close your eyes for a week for this?

Enter Sir Philip Blandford

.

Sir Philip. What has occasioned this disturbance?

Lady H. Ask that gentleman.

Sir Abel. Sir, I am accused–

Lady H. Convicted! convicted!

Sir Abel. Well, I will not argue with you about words–because I must bow to your superior practice–But, Sir–

Sir Philip. Pshaw! [*Apart.*] Lady Handy, some of your people were inquiring for you.

Lady H. Thank you, sir. Come, Sir Abel.
[*Exit.*

Sir Abel. Yes, my lady–I say [*To* Evergreen
.] cou'dn't you give me a hint of the way he had–

Lady H. [*Without.*] Sir Abel!

Sir Abel. Coming, my soul!
[*Exit.*

Sir Philip. So! you have well obeyed my orders in keeping this Henry from my presence.

Everg. I was not to blame, master.

Sir Philip. Has Farmer Ashfield left the Castle?

Everg. No, sir.

Sir Philip. Send him hither. [*Exit* Evergreen

.] That boy must be driven far, far from my sight–but where?–no matter! the world is large enough.

Enter Ashfield

.

–Come hither. I believe you hold a farm of mine.

Ash. Ees, zur, I do, at your zarvice.

Sir Philip. I hope a profitable one?

Ash. Zometimes it be, zur. But thic year it be all t'other way as 'twur–but I do hope, as our landlords have a tightish big lump of the good, they'll be zo kind hearted as to take a little bit of the bad.

Sir Philip. It is but reasonable–I conclude then you are in my debt.

Ash. Ees, zur, I be–at your zarvice.

Sir Philip. How much?

Ash. I do owe ye a hundred and fifty pounds–at your zarvice.

Sir Philip. Which you can't pay?

Ash. Not a varthing, zur–at your zarvice.

Sir Philip. Well, I am willing to give you every indulgence.

Ash. Be you, zur? that be deadly kind. Dear heart! it will make my auld dame quite young again, and I don't think helping a poor man will do your honour's health any harm–I don't indeed, zur–I had a thought of speaking to your worship about it–but then, thinks I, the gentleman, mayhap, be one of those that do like to do a good turn, and not have a word zaid about it–zo, zur, if you had not mentioned what I owed you, I am zure I never should–should not, indeed, zur.

Sir Philip. Nay, I will wholly acquit you of the debt, on condition–

Ash. Ees, zur.

Sir Philip. On condition, I say, you instantly turn out that boy–that Henry.

Ash. Turn out Henry!–Ha, ha, ha! Excuse my tittering, zur; but you bees making your vun of I, zure.

Sir Philip. I am not apt to trifle–send him instantly from you, or take the consequences.

Ash. Turn out Henry! I do vow I shou'dn't knaw how to zet about it–I should not, indeed, zur.

Sir Philip. You hear my determination. If you disobey, you know what will follow–I'll leave you to reflect on it.

[*Exit.*

Ash. Well, zur, I'll argufy the topic, and then you may wait upon me, and I'll tell ye. [*Makes the motion of turning out.*]–I shou'd be deadly awkward at it, vor zartain–however, I'll put the case–Well! I goes whiztling whoam–noa, drabbit it! I shou'dn't be able to whiztle a bit, I'm zure. Well! I goas whoam, and I zees Henry zitting by my wife, mixing up someit to comfort the wold zoul, and take away the pain of her rheumatics–Very well! Then Henry places a chair vor I by the vire zide, and says–"Varmer, the horses be fed, the sheep be folded, and you have nothing to do but to zit down, smoke your pipe, and be happy!" Very well! [*Becomes affected.*] Then I zays–"Henry, you be poor and friendless, zo you must turn out of my houze directly." Very well! then my wife stares at I–reaches her hand towards the vire place, and throws the poker at my head. Very well! then Henry gives a kind of aguish shake, and getting up, sighs from the bottom of his heart–then holding up his head like a king, zays–"Varmer, I have too long been a burden to you–Heaven protect you, as you have me–Farewell! I go." Then I says, "If thee doez I'll be domn'd!" [*With great energy.*] Hollo! you Mister Sir Philip! you may come in.–

Enter Sir Philip Blandford

.

Zur, I have argufied the topic, and it wou'dn't be pratty–zo I can't.

Sir Philip. Can't! absurd!

Ash. Well, zur, there is but another word–I wont.

Sir Philip. Indeed!

Ash. No, zur, I won't–I'd zee myself hang'd first, and you too, zur–I wou'd indeed. [*Bowing.*

Sir Philip. You refuse then to obey.

Ash. I do, zur–at your zarvice.

[*Bowing.*

Sir Philip. Then the law must take its course.

Ash. I be zorry for that too–I be, indeed, zur, but if corn wou'dn't grow I cou'dn't help it; it wer'n't poison'd by the hand that zow'd it. Thic hand, zur, be as free from guilt as your own.

Sir Philip. Oh!

[*Sighing deeply.*

Ash. It were never held out to clinch a hard bargain, nor will it turn a good lad out into the wide wicked world, because he be poorish a bit. I be zorry you be offended, zur, quite–but come what wool, I'll never hit thic hand against here, but when I be zure that zumeit at inside will jump against it with pleasure. [*Bowing.*] I do hope you'll repent of all your zins–I do, indeed, zur; and if you shou'd, I'll come and zee you again as friendly as ever–I wool, indeed, zur.

Sir Philip. Your repentance will come too late.

[*Exit.*

Ash. Thank ye, zur–Good morning to you–I do hope I have made myzel agreeable– and so I'll go whoam.

[*Exit.*

ACT THE FOURTH.

SCENE I.

A room in Ashfield's
House.

Dame Ashfield
discovered at work with her needle, Henry
sitting by her.

Dame. Come, come, Henry, you'll fret yourself ill, child. If Sir Philip will not be kind to you, you are but where you were.

Henry. [*Rising.*] My peace of mind is gone for ever. Sir Philip may have cause for hate;–spite of his unkindness to me, my heart seeks to find excuses for him–oh! that heart doats on his lovely daughter.

Dame. [*Looking out.*] Here comes Tummas home at last. Heyday what's the matter with the man! He doesn't seem to know the way into his own house.

Enter Ashfield
, *musing, he stumbles against a chair.*

Tummas, my dear Tummas, what's the matter?

Ash. [*Not attending.*] It be lucky vor he I be's zoo pratty behaved, or dom if I–[*Doubling his fist.*

Dame. Who–what?

Ash. Nothing at all; where's Henry?

Henry. Here, farmer.

Ash. Thee wouldn't leave us, Henry, wou't?

Henry. Leave you! What, leave you now, when by my exertion I can pay off part of the debt of gratitude I owe you? oh, no!

Ash. Nay, it were not vor that I axed, I promise thee; come, gi'us thy hand on't then. [*Shaking hands.*] Now, I'll tell ye. Zur Philip did send vor I about the money I do owe 'un; and said as how he'd make all straight between us——

Dame. That was kind.

Ash. Ees, deadly kind. Make all straight on condition I did turn Henry out o'my doors.

Dame. What!

Henry. Where will his hatred cease?

Dame. And what did you say, Tummas?

Ash. Why I zivelly tould un, if it were agreeable to he to behave like a brute, it were agreeable to I to behave like a man.

Dame. That was right. I wou'd have told him a great deal more.

Ash. Ah! likely. Then a' zaid I shou'd ha' a bit a laa vor my pains.

Henry. And do you imagine I will see you suffer on my account? No–I will remove this hated form—- [*Going.*]

Ash. No, but thee shat'un–thee shat'un–I tell thee. Thee have givun me thy hand on't, and dom'me if thee sha't budge one step out of this house. Drabbit it! what can he do? he can't send us to jail. Why, I have corn will zell for half the money I do owe'un–and han't I cattle and sheep? deadly lean to be zure–and han't I a thumping zilver watch, almost as big as thy head? and Dame here a got——How many silk gowns have thee got, dame!

Dame. Three, Tummas–and sell them all–and I'll go to church in a stuff one–and let Mrs. Grundy turn up her nose as much as she pleases.

Henry. Oh, my friends, my heart is full. Yet a day will come, when this heart will prove its gratitude.

Dame. That day, Henry, is every day.

Ash. Dang it! never be down hearted. I do know as well as can be, zome good luck will turn up. All the way I comed whoam I looked to vind a purse in the path. But I didn't though. [*A knocking at the door.*]

Dame. Ah! here they are, coming to sell I suppose–

Ash. Lettun–lettun zeize and zell; we ha gotten here [*Striking his breast.*] what we won't zell, and they can't zell. [*Knocking again.*] Come in–dang it, don't ye be shy.

Enter Morrington *and* Gerald

.

Henry. Ah! the strangers I saw this morning. These are not officers of law.

Ash. Noa!–Walk in, gemmen. Glad to zee ye wi' all my heart and zoul. Come, dame, spread a cloth, bring out cold meat, and a mug of beer.

Gerald. [*To* Morrington
.] That is the boy. [Morrington
nods.]

Ash. Take a chair, zur.

Mor. I thank, and admire your hospitality. Don't trouble yourself, good woman.–I am not inclined to eat.

Ash. That be the case here. To-day none o'we be auver hungry: misfortin be apt to stay the stomach confoundedly–

Mor. Has misfortune reached this humble dwelling?

Ash. Ees, zur. I do think vor my part it do work its way in every where.

Mor. Well, never despair.

Ash. I never do, zur. It is not my way. When the sun do shine I never think of voul weather, not I; and when it do begin to rain, I always think that's a zure zign it will give auver.

Mor. Is that young man your son?

Ash. No, zur–I do wish he were wi' all my heart and zoul.

Gerald. [*To* Morrington
.] Sir, remember.

Mor. Doubt not my prudencc. Young man, your appearance interests me;–how can I serve you?

Henry. By informing me who are my parents.

Mor. That I cannot do.

Henry. Then, by removing from me the hatred of Sir Philip Blandford.

Mor. Does Sir Philip hate you?

Henry. With such severity, that even now he is about to ruin these worthy creatures, because they have protected me.

Mor. Indeed! misfortune has made him cruel. That should not be.

Ash. Noa, it should not, indeed, zur.

Mor. It shall not be.

Ash. Shan't it, zur? But how shan't it?

Mor. I will prevent it.

Ash. Wool ye faith, and troth? Now, dame, did not I zay zome good luck would turn up?

Henry. Oh, sir, did I hear you rightly? Will you preserve my friends?–will you avert the cruel arm of power, and make the virtuous happy? my tears must thank you.

[*Taking his hand.*

Mor. [*Disengaging his hand.*] Young man, you oppress me–forbear! I do not merit thanks–pay your gratitude where you are sure 'tis due–to Heaven. Observe me–here is a bond of Sir Philip Blandford's for 1000*l.*–do you present it to him, and obtain a discharge for the debt of this worthy man. The rest is at your own disposal–no thanks.

Henry. But, sir, to whom am I thus highly indebted?

Mor. My name is Morrington. At present that information must suffice.

Henry. Morrington.

Ash. [*Bowing.*] Zur, if I may be so bold–

Mor. Nay, friend—-

Ash. Don't be angry, I hadn't thanked you, zur, nor I won't.–Only, zur, I were going to ax, when you wou'd call again. You shall have my stamp note vor the money, you shall, indeed, zur. And in the mean time, I do hope you'll take zomeit in way of remembrance as 'twere.

Dame. Will your honour put a couple of turkies in your pocket?

Ash. Or pop a ham under your arm? don't ye zay no, if it's agreeable.

Mor. Farewell, good friends, I shall repeat my visit soon.

Dame. The sooner the better.

Ash. Good bye to ye, zur,–Dame and I wool go to work as merry as crickets. Good bye, Henry.

Dame. Heaven bless your honour–and I hope you will carry as much joy away with you, as you leave behind you–I do indeed.

[*Exeunt* Ashfield

and Dame.

Mor. Young man, proceed to the Castle, and demand an audience of Sir Philip Blandford. In your way thither, I'll instruct you further.–Give me your hand.

[*Exeunt* Morrington

, looking stedfastly on Henry

, Gerald

following.

SCENE II.

An Apartment in the Castle.

Sir Philip Blandford

discovered–Miss Blandford

reading.

Miss B. Shall I proceed to the next essay?

Sir Philip. What does it treat of?

Miss B. Love and friendship.

Sir Philip. A satire?

Miss B. No, father;–an eulogy.

Sir Philip. Thus do we find, in the imaginations of men, what we in vain look for in their hearts.–Lay it by. [*A knocking at the door.*] Come in–

Enter Evergreen

Everg. My dear master, I am a petitioner to you.

Sir Philip. [*Rises.*] None possesses a better claim to my favour–ask, and receive.

Everg. I thank you, sir. The unhappy Henry–

Miss B. What of him?

Sir Philip. Emma, go to your apartment.

Miss B. Poor Henry!

Sir Philip. Imprudent man!

Everg. [Sir Philip
turns from hint with resentment.] Nay, be not angry; he is without, and entreats to be admitted.

Sir Philip. I cannot, will not, again behold him.

Everg. I am sorry you refuse me, as it compels me to repeat his words: "If," said he, "Sir Philip denies my humble request, tell him, I demand to see him."

Sir Philip. Demand to see me! well, his *high* command shall be obeyed then [*Sarcastically*]. Bid him approach.

[*Exit* Evergreen

Enter Henry

Sir Philip. By what title, sir, do you thus intrude on me?

Henry. By one of an imperious nature, the title of a creditor.

Sir Philip. I *your* debtor!

Henry. Yes; for you owe me justice. You, perhaps, withhold from me the inestimable treasure of a parent's blessing.

Sir Philip. [*Impatiently.*] To the business that brought you hither.

Henry. Thus then–I believe this is your signature.

[*Producing a bond.*

Sir Philip. Ah! [*Recovering himself.*] it is–

Henry. Affixed to a bond of 1000*l.* which, by assignment, is mine. By virtue of this I discharge the debt of your worthy tenant Ashfield! who, it seems, was guilty of the crime of vindicating the injured, and protecting the unfortunate. Now, Sir Philip, the retribution my hate demands is, that what remains of this obligation may not be now paid to me, but wait your entire convenience and leisure.

Sir Philip. No! that must not be.

Henry. Oh, sir! why thus oppress an innocent man?–why spurn from you a heart, that pants to serve you? No answer, farewell.

[*Going.*

Sir Philip. Hold–one word before we part–tell me–I dread to ask it [*Aside.*]–How came you possessed of this bond?

Henry. A stranger, whose kind benevolence stepped in and saved–

Sir Philip. His name?

Henry. Morrington.

Sir Philip. Fiend! tormenter! has he caught me!–You have seen this Morrington?

Henry. Yes.

Sir Philip. Did he speak of me?

Henry. He did–and of your daughter. "Conjure him," said he, "not to sacrifice the lovely Emma, by a marriage her heart revolts at. Tell him, the life and fortune of a parent are not his own; he holds them but in trust for his offspring. Bid him reflect, that, while his daughter merits the brightest rewards a father can bestow, she is by that father doomed to the harshest fate tyranny can inflict."

Sir Philip. Torture! [*With vehemence.*] Did he say who caused this sacrifice?

Henry. He told me you had been duped of your fortune by sharpers.

Sir Philip. Aye, he knows that well. Young man, mark me:–This Morrington, whose precepts wear the face of virtue, and whose practice seems benevolence, was the chief of the hellish banditti that ruined me.

Henry. Is it possible?

Sir Philip. That bond you hold in your hand was obtained by robbery.

Henry. Confusion!

Sir Philip. Not by the thief who, encountering you as a man, stakes life against life, but by that most cowardly villain, who, in the moment when reason sleeps, and passion is roused, draws his snares around you, and hugs you to your ruin.

Henry. On your soul, is Morrington that man?

Sir Philip. On my soul, he is.

Henry. Thus, then, I annihilate the act–and thus I tread upon a villain's friendship. [*Tearing the bond.*

Sir Philip. Rash boy! what have you done?

Henry. An act of justice to Sir Philip Blandford.

Sir Philip. For which you claim my thanks?

Henry. Sir, I am thanked already–here. [*Pointing to his heart.*] Curse on such wealth! compared with its possession, poverty is splendour. Fear not for me–I shall not feel the piercing cold; for in that man, whose heart beats warmly for his fellow creatures, the blood circulates with freedom–My food shall be what few of the pampered sons of greatness can boast of, the luscious bread of independence; and the opiate, that brings me sleep, will be the recollection of the day passed in innocence.

Sir Philip. Noble boy!–Oh Blandford!

Henry. Ah!

Sir Philip. What have I said?

Henry. You called me Blandford.

Sir Philip. 'Twas error–'twas madness.

Henry. Blandford! a thousand hopes and fears rush on my heart. Disclose to me my birth–be it what it may, I am your slave for ever. Refuse me, you create a foe, firm and implacable as——

Sir Philip. Ah! am I threatened? Do not extinguish the spark of pity my breast is warmed with.

Henry. I will not. Oh! forgive me.

Sir Philip. Yes, on one condition–leave me.–Ah! some one approaches. Begone, I insist–I entreat.

Henry. That word has charmed me! I obey: Sir Philip, you may hate, but you shall respect, me. [*Exit.*

Enter Handy
, *jun.*

Handy, jun. At last, thank Heaven, I have found somebody. But, Sir Philip, were you indulging in soliloquy?–You seem agitated.

Sir Philip. No, sir; rather indisposed.

Handy, jun. Upon my soul, I am devilish glad to find you. Compared with this castle, the Cretan labyrinth was intelligible; and unless some kind Ariadne gives me a clue, I shan't have the pleasure of seeing you above once a-week.

Sir Philip. I beg your pardon, I have been an inattentive host.

Handy, jun. Oh, no; but when a house is so devilish large, and the party so very small, they ought to keep together; for, to say the truth, though no one on earth feels a warmer regard for Robert Handy than I do–I soon get heartily sick of his company–whatever he may be to others, he's a cursed bore to me.

Sir Philip. Where's your worthy father?

Handy, jun. As usual, full of contrivances that are impracticable, and improvements that are retrograde; forming, altogether, a whimsical instance of the confusion of arrangement, the delay of expedition, the incommodiousness of accommodation, and the infernal trouble of endeavouring to save it–he has now a score or two of workmen about him, and intends pulling down some apartments in the east wing of the Castle.

Sir Philip. Ah! ruin!–Within there!–Fly to Sir Abel Handy–Tell him to desist! order his people, on the peril of their lives, to leave the Castle instantly! Away!

Handy, jun. Sir Philip Blandford, your conduct compels me to be serious.

Sir Philip. Oh, forbear! forbear!

Handy, jun. Excuse me, sir,–an alliance, it seems, is intended between our families, founded on ambition and interest. I wish it, sir, to be formed on a nobler basis, ingenuous friendship and mutual confidence. That confidence being withheld, I must here pause; for I should hesitate in calling that man father, who refuses me the name of friend.

Sir Philip. [*Aside.*] Ah! how shall I act?

Handy, jun. Is my demand unreasonable?

Sir Philip. Strictly just–But oh!–you know not what you ask–Do you not pity me?

Handy, jun. I do.

Sir Philip. Why then seek to change it into hate?

Handy, jun. Confidence seldom generates hate–Mistrust always.

Sir Philip. Most true.

Handy, jun. I am not impelled by curiosity to ask your friendship. I scorn so mean a motive. Believe me, sir, the folly and levity of my character proceed merely from the effervescence of my heart–you will find its substance warm, steady, and sincere.

Sir Philip. I believe it from my soul.–Yes, you shall hear my story; I will lay before your view the agony, with which this wretched bosom is loaded.

Handy, jun. I am proud of your confidence, and am prepared to receive it.

Sir Philip. Not here–let me lead you to the eastern part of the castle, my young friend–mark me: This is no common trust I repose in you; for I place my life in your hands.

Handy, jun. And the pledge I give for its security is, what alone gives value to life, my honour.

[*Exeunt.*

SCENE III.

A gloomy Gallery in the Castle–in the centre a strongly barred door.–The gallery hung with portraits.

Henry

discovered examining a particular portrait, which occupies a conspicuous situation in the gallery.

Henry. Whenever curiosity has led me to this gallery, that portrait has attracted my attention–the features are peculiarly interesting. One of the house of Blandford–Blandford—my name–perhaps my father. To remain longer ignorant of my birth, I feel impossible. There is a point when patience ceases to be a virtue–Hush! I hear footsteps–Ah! Sir Philip and another in close conversation. Shall I avoid them?–No–Shall I conceal myself, and observe them?–Curse on the base suggestion!–No–

Enter Sir Philip

and Handy

, jun.

Sir Philip. That chamber contains the mystery.

Henry. [*Aside.*] Ah!

Sir Philip. [*Turning round.*] Observe that portrait. [*Seeing* Henry

–starts.] Who's there?

Handy, jun. [*To* Henry

.] Sir, we wish to be private.

Henry. My being here, sir, was merely the effect of accident. I scorn intrusion. [*Bows.*] But the important words are spoken–that chamber contains the mystery.

[*Aside.–Exit.*

Handy, jun. Who is that youth?

Sir Philip. You there behold his father–my brother–[*Weeps.*]–I've not beheld that face these twenty years.–Let me again peruse its lineaments. [*In an agony of grief.*] Oh, God! how I loved that man!–

Handy, jun. Be composed.

Sir Philip. I will endeavour. Now listen to my story.

Handy, jun. You rivet my attention.

Sir Philip. While we were boys, my father died intestate. So I, as elder born, became the sole possessor of his fortune; but the moment the law gave me power, I divided, in equal portions, his large possessions, one of which I with joy presented to my brother.

Handy, jun. It was noble.

Sir Philip. [*With suppressed agony.*] You shall now hear, sir, how I was rewarded. Chance placed in my view a young woman of superior personal charms; my heart was captivated–Fortune she possessed not–but mine was ample. She blessed me by consenting to our union, and my brother approved my choice.

Handy, jun. How enviable your situation!

Sir Philip. Oh! [*Sighing deeply.*] On the evening previous to my intended marriage, with a mind serene as the departing sun, whose morning beam was to light me to happiness, I sauntered to a favourite tree, where, lover-like, I had marked the name of my destined bride, and, with every nerve braced to the tone of ecstasy, I was wounding the bark with a deeper impression of the name–when, oh, God!—

Handy, jun. Pray proceed.

Sir Philip. When the loved offspring of my mother, and the woman my soul adored–the only two beings on earth, who had wound themselves round my heart by every tie dear to the soul of man, placed themselves before me; I heard him–even now the sound is in my ears, and drives me to madness–I heard him breathe vows of love, which she answered with burning kisses–He pitied his poor brother, and told her he had prepared a vessel to bear her for ever from me.–They were about to depart, when the burning fever in my heart rushed upon my brain–Picture the young tiger, when first his savage nature rouses him to vengeance–the knife was in my gripe–I sprang upon them–with one hand I tore the faithless woman from his damned embrace, and with the other–stabbed my brother to the heart.

Handy, jun. The wretched woman—

Sir Philip. Was secretly conveyed here–even to that chamber.–She proved pregnant, and in giving birth to a son, paid the forfeit of her perjury by death. My task being ended, yours begins.

Handy, jun. Mine!

Sir Philip. Yes, that chamber contains evidence of my shame; the fatal instrument, with other guilty proofs, lie there concealed–can you wonder I dread to visit the scene of horror–can you wonder I implore you, in mercy, to save me from the task? Oh! my friend, enter the chamber, bury in endless night those instruments of blood, and I will kneel and worship you.

Handy, jun. I will.

Sir Philip. [*Weeps.*] Will you? [*Embraces him.*] I am unused to kindness from man, and it affects me. Oh! can you press to your guiltless heart that bloodstained hand!

Handy, jun. Sir Philip, let men without faults condemn–I must pity you.

[*Exeunt* Handy
, jun. *leading* Sir Philip
.

ACT THE FIFTH.
SCENE I.

A wooded view of the country.

Enter Susan Ashfield
, *who looks about with anxiety, and then comes forward.*

Susan. I fear my conduct is very imprudent.–Has not Mr. Handy told me he is engaged to another? But 'tis hard for the heart to forego, without one struggle, its only hope of happiness; and, conscious of my honour, what have I to fear? Perhaps he may repent of his unkindness to me–at least I'll put his passion to the proof; if he be worthy of my love, happiness is for ever mine; if not, I'll tear him from my breast, though from the wound my life's blood should follow. Ah! he comes–I feel I am a coward, and my poor alarmed heart trembles at its approaching trial–pardon me, female delicacy, if for a moment I seem to pass thy sacred limits.

[*Retires up the stage.*

Enter Handy

, *jun.*

Handy, jun. By Heavens! the misfortunes of Sir Philip Blandford weigh so heavily on my spirits, that–but confusion to melancholy! I am come here to meet an angel, who will, in a moment, drive away the blue devils like mist before the sun. Let me again read the dear words; [*Reading a letter.*] "I confess, I love you still;" [*Kisses the letter.*] but I dare not believe their truth till her sweet lips confirm it. Ah! she's there–Susan, my angel! a thousand thanks. A life of love can alone repay the joy your letter gave me.

Susan. Do you not despise me?

Handy, jun. No; love you more than ever.

Susan. Oh! Robert, this is the very crisis of my fate.——From this moment we meet with honour, or we meet no more. If we must part, perhaps, when you lead your happy bride to church, you may stumble over your Susan's grave. Well, be it so.

Handy, jun. Away with such sombre thoughts!

Susan. Tell me my doom–yet hold–you are wild, impetuous–you do not give your heart fair play–therefore promise me (perhaps 'tis the last favour I shall ask), that before you determine whether our love shall die or live with honour, you will remain here alone a few moments, and that you will give those moments to reflection.

Handy, jun. I do–I will.

Susan. With a throbbing heart I will wait at a little distance. May virtuous love and sacred honour direct his thoughts!

[*Aside.–Exit.*

Handy, jun. Yes, I will reflect, that I am the most fortunate fellow in England. She loves me still–what is the consequence?–that love will triumph–that she will be mine–mine without the degradation of marriage–love, pride, all gratified–how I shall be envied when I triumphantly pass the circles of fashion! One will cry, "Who is that angel?"–another, "Happy fellow!" then Susan will smile around–will she smile? oh yes–she will be all gaiety–mingle with the votaries of pleasure, and–what! Susan Ashfield the companion of licentious women!–Damnation!–no! I wrong her–she would not–she would rather shun society–she would be melancholy–melancholy! [*Sighs, and looks at his watch.*]–would the time were over!–Pshaw! I think of it too seriously–'Tis false–I do not.–Should her virtue yield to love, would not remorse affect her health? should I not behold that lovely form sicken and decay–perhaps die?–die! then what am I?–a villain, loaded with her parents' curses and my own.–Let me fly from the dreadful thought.–But how fly from it?–[*Calmly.*]–By placing before my imagination a picture of more honourable lineaments.–I make her my wife.–Ah! then she would smile on me–there's rapture in the thought;–instead of vice producing decay, I behold virtue emblazoning beauty; instead of Susan on the bed of death, I behold her giving to my hopes a dear pledge of our mutual love. She places it in my arms–down her father's honest face runs a tear–but 'tis the tear of joy. Oh, this will be luxury! paradise!–Come, Susan!–come, my love, my soul–my *wife*.

Enter Susan

–she at first hesitates–on hearing the word wife, *she springs into his arms.*

Susan. Is it possible?

Handy, jun. Yes, those charms have conquered.

Susan. Oh! no; do not so disgrace the victory you have gained–'tis your own virtue that has triumphed.

Handy, jun. My Susan! how true it is that fools alone are vicious. But let us fly to my father, and obtain his consent. On recollection, that may not be quite so easy. His arrangements with Sir Philip Blandford are–are–not mine, so there's an end of that. And Sir Philip, by misfortune, knows how to appreciate happiness. Then poor Miss Blandford–upon my soul I feel for her.

Susan. [*Ironically.*] Come, don't make yourself miserable. If my suspicions be true, she'll not break her heart for your loss.

Handy, jun. Nay, don't say so; she will be unhappy.

Ash. [*Without.*] There he is. Dame, shall I shoot at un?

Dame. No.

Susan. My father's voice.

Ash. Then I'll leather un wi' my stick.

Enter Ashfield

and Dame

.

Ash. What do thee do here with my Sue, eh?

Handy, jun. With your Sue!–she's mine–mine by a husband's right.

Ash. Husband! what, thee Sue's husband?

Handy, jun. I soon shall be.

Ash. But how tho'?–What! faith and troth?–What! like as I married Dame?

Handy, jun. Yes.

Ash. What! axed three times!

Handy, jun. Yes; and from this moment I'll maintain, that the real temple of love is a parish church–Cupid is a chubby curate–his torch is the sexton's lantern–and the according pæan of the spheres is the profound nasal thorough bass of the clerk's Amen.

Ash. Huzza! only to think now–my blessing go with you, my children!

Dame. And mine.

Ash. And Heaven's blessing too. Ecod, I believe now, as thy feyther zays, thee canst do every thing!

Handy, jun. No; for there is one thing I cannot do–injure the innocence of woman.

Ash. Drabbit it! I shall walk in the road all day to zee Sue ride by in her own coach.

Susan. You must ride with me, father.

Dame. I say, Tummas, what will Mrs. Grundy say then?

Ash. I do hope thee will not be asham'd of thy feyther in laa, wool ye?

Handy, jun. No; for then I must also be ashamed of myself, which I am resolved not to be again.

Enter Sir Abel Handy

Sir Abel. Heyday, Bob! why an't you gallanting your intended bride? but you are never where you ought to be.

Handy, jun. Nay, sir, by your own confession I *am* where I ought to be.

Sir Abel. No! you ought to be at the Castle–Sir Philip is there, and Miss Blandford is there, and Lady Handy is there, and therefore–

Handy, jun. You are *not* there. In one word, I shall not marry Miss Blandford.

Sir Abel. Indeed! who told you so?

Handy, jun. One who never lies–and, therefore, one I am determined to make a friend of–my conscience.

Sir Abel. But zounds! sir, what excuse have you?

Handy, jun. [*Taking* Susan's hand.] A very fair one, sir–is not she?

Sir Abel. Why, yes, sir, I can't deny it–but, 'sdeath, sir, this overturns my best plan!

Handy, jun. No, sir; for a parent's best plan is his son's happiness, and that it will establish. Come, give us your consent. Consider how we admire all your wonderful inventions.

Sir Abel. No, not my plough, Bob–but 'tis a devilish clever plough.

Handy, jun. I dare say it is. Come, sir, consent, and perhaps, in our turn, we may invent something that may please you.

Sir Abel. He! he! he! well–but hold–what's the use of my consent without my wife's–bless you! I dare no more approve, without–

Enter Gerald

Gerald. Health to this worthy company!

Sir Abel. The same to you, sir.

Handy, jun. Who have we here, I wonder?

Gerald. I wish to speak with Sir Abel Handy.

Sir Abel. I am the person.

Gerald. You are married?

Sir Abel. Damn it! he sees it in my face.–Yes, I have that happiness.

Gerald. Is it a happiness?

Sir Abel. To say the truth–why do you ask?

Gerald. I want answers, not questions–and depend on't 'tis your interest to answer me.

Handy, jun. An extraordinary fellow this!

Gerald. Would it break your heart to part with her!

Sir Abel. Who are you, sir, that——

Gerald. Answers–I want answers–would it break your heart, I ask?

Sir Abel. Why, not absolutely, I hope. Time, and philosophy, and——

Gerald. I understand–what sum of money wou'd you give to the man, who would dissolve your marriage contract?

Handy, jun. He means something, sir.

Sir Abel. Do you think so, Bob?

Gerald. Would you give a thousand pounds?

Sir Abel. No!

Handy, jun. No!

Sir Abel. No; I would not give one; but I would give five thousand pounds.

Gerald. Generously offered–a bargain–I'll do it.

Sir Abel. But, an't you deceiving me?

Gerald. What should I gain by that?

Sir Abel. Tell me your name?

Gerald. Time will tell that.

Lady H. [*Without.*] Sir Abel, where are you?

Gerald. That's your wife's voice–I know it.

Sir Abel. So do I.

Gerald. I'll wait without–Cry, "Hem!" when you want me.

Sir Abel. Then you need not go far–

[*Exit* Gerald

I dare not believe it–I should go out of my wits–and then if he fail, what a pickle I shall be in! Here she is.

Enter Lady Handy

Lady H. So, sir, I have found you at last?

Handy, jun. My honoured mamma, you have just come in time to give your consent to my marriage with my sweet Susan.

Lady H. And do you imagine I will agree to such degradation?

Ash. Do'e, Lady Nelly, do'e be kind hearted to the young loviers.–Remember how I used to let thee zit up all night a sweethearting.

Lady H. Silence! and have you dared to consent?

[*To* Sir Abel

Sir Abel. Oh, no, my Lady!

Handy, jun. Sir, you had better cry–"Hem."

Sir Abel. I think it's time, Bob–Hem!

Handy, jun. Hem!

Lady H. What do you mean by–Hem!

Sir Abel. Only, my dear, something troublesome I want to get rid of–Hem!

Enter Gerald

There he is–never was so frightened in all my life.

[Gerald

advances.]

Lady H. [*Shrieks and exclaims.*] Gerald!

Gerald. Yes.

Lady H. An't you dead, Gerald? Twenty years away and not dead?

Gerald. No, wife.

Sir Abel. Wife! did you say, wife?

Gerald. Yes.

Sir Abel. Say it again.

Gerald. She is my wife.

Sir Abel. Once more.

Gerald. My lawful, wedded wife.

Sir Abel. Oh, my dear fellow!–Oh, my dear boy! Oh, my dear girl!–[*Embraces* Gerald *and the rest.*] Oh, my dear! [*Running to* Mrs. Gerald .] No–yes, now she an't my wife, I will–well–how will you have the five thousand? Will you have it in cash, or in bank notes–or stocks, or India bonds, or lands, or patents, or——

Gerald. No–land will do–I wish to kill my own mutton.

Sir Abel. Sir, you shall kill all the sheep in Hampshire.

Gerald. Sir Abel, you have lost five thousand pounds, and with it, properly managed, an excellent wife, who, though I cannot condescend to take again as mine– you may depend on't shall never trouble you. Come! this way [*Beckoning to* Mrs. Gerald .]–important events now call on me, and prevent my staying longer with this company. Sir Abel, we shall meet soon. Nay, come, you know I'm not used to trifle; Come, come–[*She reluctantly, but obediently, crosses the stage, and runs off*–Gerald *follows.*]

Sir Abel. [*Imitating.*] Come, come–That's a damn'd clever fellow! Joy, joy, my boy! Here, here, your hands–The first use I make of liberty, is to give happiness–I wish I had more imitators–Well, what will you do? [*Walks about exultingly.*] Where will you go? I'll go any where you like–Will you go to Bath, or Brighton, or Petersburgh, or Jerusalem, or Seringapatam? all the same to me–we single fellows–we rove about– nobody cares about us–we care for nobody.

Handy, jun. I must to the Castle, father.

Sir Abel. Have with you Bob. [*Singing.*] "I'll sip every flower–I'll change every hour."–[*Beckoning.*]–Come, come–[*Exeunt* Sir Abel , Handy , *jun. and* Susan . Susan *kisses her hand to* Ashfield *and* Dame .]

Ash. Bless her! how nicely she do trip it away with the gentry!

Dame. And then, Tummas, think of the wedding.

Ash. [*Reflecting.*] I declare I shall be just the zame as ever–may be I may buy a smartish bridle, or a zilver backy stopper, or the like o' that.

Dame. [*Apart.*] And, then, when we come out of church, Mrs. Grundy will be standing about there–

Ash. I shall shake hands agreeably wi' all my friends. [*Apart.*]

Dame. [*Apart.*] Then I just look at her in this manner.

Ash. [*Apart.*] How dost do, Peter–Ah, Dick,–glad to zee thee wi' all my zoul. [*Bows towards the centre of the stage.*]

Dame. [*Apart.*] Then, with a kind of half curt'sy, I shall–[*She advances to the centre also, and their heads meet.*]

Ash. What an wold fool thee be'st, Dame–Come along, and behave pratty, do'e. [*Exeunt.*

SCENE II.

The same as act fourth, scene third.

Enter Handy

, jun. with caution, bearing a light, and a large key.

Handy, jun. Now to fulfil my promise with Sir Philip Blandford–by–entering that chamber, and removing–'Tis rather awful–I don't half like it, somehow, every thing is so cursedly still. What's that? I thought I heard something–no–why, 'sdeath, I am not afraid–no–I'm quite su–su–sure of that–only every thing is so cursedly hush, and–[*A flash of light, and a tremendous explosion takes place.*] What the devil's that? [*Trembling.*] I swear I hear some one–lamenting–who's there?

Enter Sir Abel Handy

.

Father? [*Trembling.*]

Sir Abel. [*Trembling.*] Bob!

Handy, jun. Have you seen any thing!

Sir Abel. Oh, my dear boy!

Handy, jun. Damn it, don't frighten one–

Sir Abel. Such an accident! Mercy on us!

Handy, jun. Speak!

Sir Abel. I was mixing the ingredients of my grand substitute for gunpowder, when somehow it blew up, and set the curtains on fire, and–

Handy, jun. Curtains! zounds, the room's in a blaze.

Sir Abel. Don't say so, Bob.

Handy, jun. What's to be done? Where's your famous preparation for extinguishing flames?

Sir Abel. It is not mixed.

Handy, jun. Where's your fire escape?

Sir Abel. It is not fixed.

Handy, jun. Where's your patent fire engine?

Sir Abel. 'Tis on the road.

Handy, jun. Well, you are never at a loss.

Sir Abel. Never.

Handy, jun. What's to be done?

Sir Abel. I don't know. I say, Bob, I have it–perhaps it will go out of itself!

Handy, jun. Go out! it increases every minute–Let us run for assistance–Let us alarm the family. [*Exit.*

Sir Abel. Yes–dear me! dear me!

Servant. [*Without.*] Here, John! Thomas! some villain has set fire to the Castle. If you catch the rascal, throw him into the flames.

[Sir Abel

runs off, and the alarm bell rings.

SCENE III.

The Garden of the Castle–The effects of the fire shown on the foliage and scenery.

Enter Henry

, *meeting* Evergreen

.

Henry. The Castle in flames! What occasioned it?

Everg. Alas! I know not!

Henry. Are the family in safety?

Everg. Sir Philip is.

Henry. And his daughter?

Everg. Poor lady! I just now beheld her looking with agony from that window!

Henry. Ah! Emma in danger!–Farewell!

Everg. [*Holding him.*] Are you mad? the great staircase is in flames.

Henry. I care not! Should we meet no more, tell Sir Philip I died for his daughter!

Everg. Yet reflect.

Henry. Old man, do not cling to me thus–'Sdeath! men will encounter peril to ruin a woman, and shall I hesitate when it is to save one?

[*Exit.*

Everg. Brave, generous boy! Heaven preserve thee!

Enter Sir Philip Blandford

.

Sir Philip. Emma, my child, where art thou?

Everg. I fear, sir, the Castle will be destroyed.

Sir Philip. My child! my child! where is she? speak!

Everg. Alas! she remains in the Castle!

Sir Philip. Ah; then will I die with her! [*Going.*

Everg. Hold, dear master! if human power can preserve her, she is safe–The bravest, noblest of men has flown to her assistance.

Sir Philip. Heaven reward him with its choicest blessings!

Everg. 'Tis Henry.

Sir Philip. Henry! Heaven will reward him–I will reward him!

Everg. Then be happy; Look, sir!

Sir Philip. Ah! dare I trust my eyes!

Everg. He bears her safe in his arms.

Sir Philip. Bountiful Creator, accept my thanks!

Enter Henry

, *bearing* Emma

in his arms.

Henry. There is your daughter.

Sir Philip. My child! my Emma, revive!

Henry. [*Apart.*] Aye–now to unfold the mystery–The avenue to the eastern wing is still passable–the chamber not yet in flames–the present moment lost, and all is closed for ever. I will be satisfied, or perish.

[*Exit.*

Miss B. Am I restor'd to my dear father's arms?

Sir Philip. Yes, only blessing of my life! In future thy wishes shall be mine–thy happiness my joy.

Enter Handy

, *jun. and* Susan

.

Handy, jun. My dear friend safe! and the lovely Emma in his arms! Then let the bonfire blaze.

Sir Philip. But, Emma, where is your Henry? I wish to be just to him–I wish to thank him.

Miss B. He has withdrawn, to avoid our gratitude.–

Everg. No–he again rushed into the Castle, exclaiming, "I will penetrate that chamber, or perish in the attempt."

Sir Philip. Then all is discovered.

Handy, jun. Hush, for Heaven's sake collect yourself!

Enter Henry

, *in great agitation.*

Miss B. Ah! [*Shrieks.*] Thank Heaven, he's safe! What urged you, Henry, again to venture in the Castle?

Henry. Fate! the desperate attempt of a desperate man!

Sir Philip. Ah!

Henry. Yes; the mystery is developed. In vain the massy bars, cemented with their cankerous rust, opposed my entrance–in vain the heated suffocating damps enveloped me–in vain the hungry flames flashed their vengeance round me! What could oppose a man struggling to know his fate? I forced the doors, a firebrand was my guide, and among many evidences of blood and guilt, I found–these! [*Produces a knife and bloody cloth.*]

Sir Philip. [*Starts with horror, then, with solemnity.*] It is accomplished! Just Heaven, I bend to thy decree!–Blood must be paid by blood! Henry, that knife aimed by this fatal hand, murdered thy father!

Henry. Ah! [*Grasping the knife.*]

Miss B. [*Placing herself between him and her father.*] Henry! [*He drops his hand.*] Oh, believe him not! 'Twas madness! I've heard him talk thus wildly in his dreams! We are all friends! None will repeat his words–I'm sure none will! My heart will break!–Oh, Henry! will you destroy my father?

Henry. Would I were in my grave!

Enter Gerald

.

Sir Philip. Ah, Gerald here! How vain concealment! Well, come you to give evidence of my shame?

Gerald. I come to announce one, who for many years has watched each action of your life.

Sir Philip. Who?

Gerald. Morrington.

Sir Philip. I shall then behold the man who has so long avoided me—-

Gerald. But ever has been near you–he is here.

Enter Morrington
, wrapped up in his cloak.

Sir Philip. Well, behold your victim in his last stage of human wretchedness! Come you to insult me;

[Morrington
clasps his hands together, and hides his face.]

Ah! can even you pity me? Speak–still silent–still mysterious–Well, let me employ what remains of life, in thinking of hereafter–[*Addressing Heaven.*] Oh, my brother! we soon shall meet again–And let me hope, that, stripped of those passions which make men devils, I may receive the heavenly balm of thy forgiveness, as I, from my inmost soul, do pardon thee.

[Morrington
becomes convulsed with agony, and falls into Gerald's
arms.]

Ah! what means that agony? He faints! give him air!

[*They throw open his cloak and hat.*]

[*Starts.*] Angels of mercy! my brother! 'tis he! he lives! Henry, support your father!

Henry. [*Running to* Morrington
.] Ah, my father! he revives!

Sir Philip. Hush!

[Morrington
recovers–seeing his brother, covers his face with shame, then falls at his feet.]

Mor. Crawling in the dust, behold a repentant wretch!–

Sir Philip. [*Indignantly.*] My brother Morrington!

Mor. Turn not away–in mercy hear me!

Sir Philip. Speak!

Mor. After the dreadful hour that parted us, agonized with remorse, I was about to punish home what your arm had left unaccomplished; when some angel whispered– "Punishment is life, not death–Live and atone!"

Sir Philip. Oh! go on!

Mor. I flew to you–I found you surrounded by sharpers–What was to be done? I became Morrington! littered with villains! practised the arts of devils! braved the assassin's steel! possessed myself of your large estates–lived hateful to myself, detested by mankind–to do what? to save an injured brother from destruction, and lay his fortune at his feet! [*Places parchments before* Sir Philip
.]

Sir Philip. Ah! is it possible!

Lightning Source UK Ltd.
Milton Keynes UK
UKOW052331300113

205633UK00001B/216/P